I0203008

Educational Technology Integration Foundations

By Mark Page-Botelho

© 2012 Mark Page-Botelho Publications. All rights reserved. ISBN 978-0-578-10774-5

Table of Contents

Below are some suggested basic ideas and rubrics to help you assess the Information Literacy *ISTE's NETS benchmarks. I purposely left the rubrics very basic to give each of you a wider berth in how you teach the skills. Please list specifics within

Introduction

Welcome, I hope you will take the time to explore my technology thoughts and concepts to see what both teachers and students are learning in in schools. Throughout this book you can find information of theory and practice of technology integration.

Key Tenet of the Integrationist

To better serve teachers, students and parents.

Analog Lives in a Digital Age

The main focus of a Technology Coordinator and teachers is to move students and parents living analog lives into the digital age. The world is rapidly changing and if schools want to help students to be competitive in the new world markets, they will need all the tools available to them. Parents are also a major component to this movement to the digital age and are often forgotten in the process.

A True Technology Enabled Classroom

"simply having access to computers and using them does not necessarily mean they are improving student learning" -Michael McGlade

What does a true technology classroom look like? With all the hard work going into creating students who are able to utilize technology, very few classrooms today actually accomplish true integration. That is why we have technology coordinators and integrationists. The front line for creating such a classroom lies with the teachers, many of whom are themselves not able to use the vast amount of tools available. In addition, the technology itself is not standardized and often is not made for use in schools. Time almost always becomes an issue, preventing or discouraging teachers from using technology today. Having a technology integrationist on staff can help alleviate many of these issues.

Oftentimes integrationists focus solely on hardware or software solutions, spending most of their effort in training teachers basic 101 skills. Over exuberant excitement for the latest greatest new gizmo without any regard to the potential,positive and negative effects can lead to waste, of time, money, and effort. Best practice is usually the casualty of integrationists that don't take the time to study the needs or potential needs of their clients. Nets for students should be used for scaffolding for technology integration. Parents are an important component to the program,as well as parents. Technology is about using new and proven technologies to support core curriculum in classrooms. However, an integrationist role also involves teaching and supporting students, parents, and teachers with skill sets and social expectations regarding the use of technology.

A true technology enabled classroom, would begin with having students well versed in acceptable use of technology in every aspect including social skills. Throughout the year lessons and projects would seamlessly use aspects of technology where the focus is solely on the core subject matter without the need of instruction for the use of the technology tools and skills.

"Technology integration is not about learning to use a computer, it's about using a computer to learn." -Amy J. Mayer

Students and teachers would already have the skill background needed for its use. Projects would be categorized into three groupings. Basic, intermediate, and difficult giving students different amount of exposure and giving the teachers room to deal with time constraints.

Key Components to Technology Integration

In order to have a successful program there are three components that must be considered. Professional Development and Integration, Professionalism Communication & Presence, and Accessibility and Availability are vital to any program.
- Professional Development and Integration, or PDI
  - Core Units of Integration for Staff, Students, and Parents
- Professionalism Communication & Presence
  - Treating Staff, Students, and Parents with Respect in an environment where they feel safe
- Accessibility and Availability
  - Being a close as possible to the client
  - Always being readily available

Professional Development and Integration
Having a program where staff and parents both have input as to the needs of the school and what should be taught to everyone involved. Things to watch out for include the new and hottest gear and programs. Also, the dreaded 101 classes of non-curriculum tied in workshops.

Professionalism Communication & Presence
Treating teachers with respect and honoring their wisdom about what they need and would like help on is often a problem with many programs. Giving teachers choice and asking them what they would personally like help on, if anything, gives them a sense of respect that will go a long way in motivating or having them appreciate and use the integrationist.

Accessibility and Availability
Being near the front lines is important. Distance is relative. If teachers don't take use of integrationists, reevaluate the location and proximity of where they are located. When a teacher is busy, they will often not go out of their way to get help, but make do. The art of teaching requires to make do without.

Useful Resources

- **Children's _Online_ Privacy _Rule COPPA_**
  - Privacy concerns for students and parents.
- **_CyberSMART_**
  - K-12 comprehensive technology curriculum. Free, easy, and ready to use. No technology experience necessary.
- **_Common Sense_**
  - Parent organization for CyberSMART, and they have their own K-12 curriculum.
- **_ISTE_ International Society for Technology in Education**
  - The most widely used standards and benchmarks world-wide. Their standards and benchmarks are extremely easy to understand and use even by people with little to no technology experience. They have separate standards for administrators, teachers, and students.

Collective Knowledge

No matter how experienced the integrationist, the collective knowledge of students and teachers is far greater.
- Integrationist should learn from and share what the staff and students know with others.
- Integrationist is the conduit of technology knowledge, a collector and voice for what works.
- Find and help students and teachers share their skills and knowledge with others.

Classroom Setup

There are many basic fundamentals that need to be thought of prior to students arriving.
1. Student accounts, each school needs to plan how students will access the Internet and local resources. Typically students should have individual logins with private storage space dedicated to saving their work throughout the year. Early year students kindergarten and first grades normally should have a class account for ease of use.
2. Software that will be used needs to be verified to run on the computer systems at hand. Additionally, all software should be checked for compatibility with classroom computers.
3. Making sure that the classroom or lab is comfortable for students is important. If your room has hard floors, have a carpet brought in for a place for students to sit during instructions and demonstration.
4. Desks with keyboard drawers is very handy, especially when students are learning to touch type.

Have name check-off slips made. These are a great way to get to know the students. Also, it helps you keep track of their progress on basic skills such as typing.

Content Filtering

There is no easy way out of keeping students safe while using online tools. Parents rightfully have an expectation that their children remain safe and are not adversely affected by using online tools. The dangers for students are numerous and many teachers have little to no idea of what the dangers are and how to protect their students from them. Everyone seems to be looking for the easy way out when dealing with cyber safety.

The magic bullet, the end all solution, or catch phrase that will allow them to blindly use technology and to have an easy excuse where no one is to blame if something goes wrong. The dangers range from cyberbullying using social media, to inadvertently viewing adult content that immediately changes the emotional character of the viewing child. The simplest act of using YouTube or a Google Image search is enough to change a child's life forever in an instant. Teachers really need to ask themselves "what if it was my child?"

Teachers lack of knowledge including the potential pitfalls of online use, and not taking the time to learn about and teach proper use takes training. It's not only the teachers that need training but also parents and the students themselves. In addition, the technology coordinators need training to work with the network administrators in configuring the network proxy, and system configurations, not to limit, but protect students.

Many coordinators will often take the "easy" approach and state that the Internet shouldn't be filtered. What they don't understand is that content is already filtered in school settings. Adult magazines are not present in school libraries, and students are supervised throughout the day. This is not to say that we need to spend our time policing students. Having a well written and thoughtful acceptable use policy is part of any school technology program. The Internet was not designed for children, but for everyone, including those who can care less about children. The pornography industry is one of the largest segments on the Internet today. Children are children in that they are innocent and we as their guardians need to practice due diligence when letting them use online based tools. Just don't fall for the easy way out catch phrases thrown around by those not wanting to learn and teach about the potential pitfalls that await online.

Assessment

Assessment for technology integration can be thought of as having two types. The first type of assessment deals with basic skills. Usually the best method of assessing basic skills is to use an observational assessment. The second type is where knowledge is assessed. It is better to use a rubric where one can be specific as to the particular knowledge or skill that need to be assessed.

Parental Feedback is important to give out often. This way parents can be kept up to date as to the ideas that their children are being exposed to. Parents can then be involved in their child's learning and may be able to contribute.

Keeping data on a student's performance can only help when it is time to make a decision at reporting time. Whether a school uses narratives, or a basic numeric scale for grading, the more data to make an informed decision the better.

For each benchmark assessed, there should be at least three assessments made.

Keeping good records is a best practice that should be high priority. There are many reasons for keeping good records such as , evidence, and it makes reporting on a student's progress valid and meaningful. No one person can possibly keep track of a student's progress in their head, so write it down!

Using standards and benchmarks makes reporting a little difficult for many teachers to conceptualize. One method that works best is to make a determination or grade each occurrence of a particular benchmark or standard. Keeping track of all of the occurrences is important. Theoretically if a child can achieve a standard should justify a pass. However, multiple attempts should be taken into consideration, since each performance of a skill or concept being observed can deviate depending on the teacher, lesson, emotional state of child, and so forth. The **ability to consistently perform** is the goal for each and every standard and benchmark.

The term "grade" is also considered a bad word in many educators mind, but once again everyone "grades." Even comment based report cards assign a level or "grade" to the performance of students. So keep track of your grades as they come in handy when making a final determination of a student's progress.

Assessment Levels
Most projects or lessons, especially skill based projects, don't always need a precise grading language. However, the language used to describe the grades can be made more specific to include skills or objects that need to be addressed.

> **Concerns**: Student is unable to start or continue without direct instruction. Little to no evidence of understanding of concept(s). Takes a reclusive role in task.

Approaching: Occasionally needs instruction to finish task. Evidence that student is starting to grasp concept(s). Takes an passive role in task.

Proficient: Clear and easy to understand all required tasks are fulfilled. Able to convey understanding of concept(s). Takes an passive role in task.

Exceeds: Elaborated or added personal connections or elements that go above and beyond required task. Full understanding of concept(s) and able to elaborate. Takes an active role in task.

Behavior Management

Getting & Maintaining Student Attention

The best method that I have found is having students turn-off their monitors whenever I need the full group attention. This method works the best as you only need one audible prompt and once completed there are no visual distractions for students. The monitors-off strategies starts off by telling students "monitors off!" Once the monitors are off, students are not to touch their mice nor their keyboards. If a particular student doesn't hear the audible prompt, they will more than likely see that their neighbor has done so and they usually follow suit.

Have students practice the monitors-off strategy to ensure smooth sailing in class.

Basic Problem Resolution

If there is a discipline problem in class, students are to be reminded to stay on task. If they continue to not follow instructions, they are to be seated on the carpeted area for a few minutes to reflect on their behavior. Talk with them once they have had time to reflect and see if they are ready to participate, if so allow them to continue the task at hand.

Google Apps

Highlights
- Docs: Sharing, Revision History
- Calendar: Sharing
- Email: Organizing, Priority, Folders, Syncing
- Forms: Data Collection

Hardware

Extra Miscellaneous Hardware

If you are teaching a block class or have a homeroom, have students by a pair of headphones and a USB flash drive. These items are good to have on hand as some classes many not have the equipment on hand. Both of these devices have benefits that students can use for many years.
- Headphones can make a work environment much more pleasant.

- Headphones are cheap and are more hygienic when used by only one person.
- USB Drives are cheap
- USB Drives can save personal work if networks are down, or computer issues arise.

Form Follows Function

It is important to have the right hardware in a lab to make lessons run smoothly. Often schools make purchasing decisions based on the latest and greatest thing to hit the market, with no consideration to what is actually needed. The iPad explosion is a great example. Form must follow function if a school wants to use their funding in a responsible way. Look at the needs first when making purchasing decisions.

Below are some consideration when choosing hardware for a static or mobile lab.

Headphones: Every computer should have headphones, which are used often when using computers. They are used for recording voice, and to listen to media. Having comfortable headphones is important, but choosing a set that can be easily cleaned is also an important factor.

Mice: Choosing an appropriately sized mouse for the size hand is often overlooked in computer labs. If you are teaching younger students, try out a laptop sized mouse. They will fit smaller hands much better than the stock mice that come with workstations. I found that corded mice work best as they won't get knocked down on the floor, and they don't require batteries. Also, they tend to be more responsive than wireless mice.

Desktops Devices

Desktops are an optimal choice if the school needs to use a powerful program. They are cheap and powerful. Desktops are always far more **powerful** and **faster** than any other device due to the fact that they use high voltage components since they have an unlimited supply of power. Also, having at least one desktop lab in reserve is handy as sometimes laptops are problematic and may not be available. Also, during PD days a lab can be used by guests or for teacher workshops.

Laptops Devices

Laptops are somewhat mobile as they can be moved from class to class. They are slower than a desktop as they use ULV (ultra low voltage) or LV (low voltage) components. Laptops are the best option for a fast multimedia web experience, far faster than chromebook, netbook, or tablet. There are different strategies for using laptops depending on the funding available. Schools can run a one-to-one program, where students each get a laptop for their use. The laptops can be purchased from the families to help offset the cost, or can be bought by the school and assigned a laptop for use throughout the year. Another option is to have students share laptops by using carts which are shared among classrooms. This is a good strategy for schools with limited funds. Buying netbooks is also a great option as they are very affordable and can do everything a full fledged laptop can do.

Netbooks & Chromebook Devices

For schools that have limited funding, but would still like students to have an all around computing device, netbooks and chromebooks are a great option. Netbooks are nothing more than a very affordable laptop that is smaller in size and still is able to do most things that a laptop can do. What makes them a better choice than a tablet is that they are multi-user and can easily be integrated into any network. This allows for easy management in an enterprise environment. In addition they are very inexpensive allowing for all students to have one. The only drawback is that they are slower than laptops.

Chromebooks are very inexpensive. They are essentially a tablet without the touch screen, but without the high cost. They use Google's Chrome browser as their operating system. They are light, have a keyboard, and have a long battery life. They are ideal for students in a school that uses Google Apps environment, or primarily use online tools. They can only do what can be done in a web browser. So movie making is out, unless a subscription to a movie making online site is purchased.

Tablet Devices

If planning to invest in a tablet form factor finding a use that is specific to the tablet form factor and function is important. Otherwise buying a laptop or investing in desktops will probably be more beneficial in that they can be used for more functions. Tablets are great for younger students who really don't need to learn about computers themselves, but rather use technology for consumption.

Younger students also are more adept in the early years at using their fingers and are not coordinated enough to use a mouse or keyboard. With that said, younger students can learn to use mice and keyboards and should be exposed to their use.

Older students can benefit from tablets when away from campus and need to write notes or gather information and take digital images or videos. It is a perfect companion device for data collection.

What makes a tablet different than a laptop,
- Super mobile
- Touch interface
- A little smaller in size than a netbook
- GPS
- Accelerometer

They are great when coupled with one of the above listed items and one or more of the following,
- Voice recording
- Image capture (video and still)
- Object manipulation via touch

Cons: (http://ipadeducators.ning.com/profiles/blogs/what-do-students-think-of)
- Slowest at of all devices
- Need to buy additional basic functions such as print and browsing of networks, which are free on laptops
- Pinch and zoom becomes tiring after awhile
- Touch interface difficult to copy and paste
- lack of digital textbook subscriptions
- lack of windows while doing research
- lack of Flash (iPad), many sites still use it
- Interface just as hard to master as desktop
- typing is cumbersome
- not as useful when in shared environment (single user)
- Currently expensive
- Still needs to be seated for classroom management, defeats purpose of mobility

Materials

Regular pencils for worksheets, or for signing names on printouts.

A computer lab often has to have other things in it other than computers. Many lessons may not even involve using a computer. While other lessons may need support material such as books from the library.

Keep a stock of coloring pencils or crayons in your room. These come especially handy if the computers go offline for whatever reason. Also, curriculum such as CyberSMART often have lessons where students need to draw.

Make sure you have a classroom supply of printing paper. Not only will you often need to replenish the printer, but you can use the paper for coloring, or for alternative assignments for students who lose their computer use privileges.

Having a portable whiteboard is a great addition, even for classrooms with overhead projector or document cameras. Sometimes a quick doodle on a whiteboard can help visual learners like no other medium.

Posters

Having posters in the computer lab or classroom is a simple way to help remind students of rules, processes, and hard to remember skills. Place them liberally throughout the classroom. Use posters in the front of the classroom primarily for student use. Place posters of ideas or things that you may have trouble remembering to remind students of in the the back of the classroom so you can see them while standing at the front of the room.

Project Process

When having students work on any type of project, a procedure should be followed to insure that students do a thorough job. The procedure is essentially no different than a standard writing process. The writing process along with the writing traits is a great combination for a project procedure for all technology projects. A solid choice for a writing traits to model after is the 6+1 Trait® Writing Model of Instruction & Assessment, Copyright © 2010 Education Northwest, http://educationnorthwest.org/traits. Any writing process model will work, but the Education Northwest has many great resources that can help one understand the concepts better.

When adapting the writing process with the writing traits for a procedure to make technology lesson or projects, very little has to be done for adoption as most projects should have content and a writing component. All that has to be done is to post the project process on a wall for to help remind students about each step in the process. The home room teachers should be teaching the writing process and traits in their classrooms, but you should remind and review them before each major project.

Projecting

There are many way to project images and video, which are important ways in which can help differentiate teaching in your classroom.
- DLP projectors are intended for video. They are not best text display.
- LCD projectors are intended for text display and are adequate for video.
- Short throw projectors are expensive but are excellent for document cameras or SmartBoards.

Tip: When using a projector in conjunction with displaying a computer desktop, use the magnifying glass function on both Macs and Windows. This really helps students to visually focus on the area of the screen that is critical to follow, as desktops usually have many distractions.

Software

Teaching technology should be about using tools available to help create. We as teachers should not be teaching how to use technology for the sake of learning how to use it as a tool only. There are circumstances where lessons will need to be thought in which the bulk of the lesson is teaching the use of a technology tool, but that is to be expected. However, with the rapidly changing world of technology and its innovations, we should be more concerned with using technology only as a tool or path to a meaningful end.

Considerations in Choice
- Try to choose programs that can be used in other classrooms or through the years. This allows students to become proficient in its use and other teachers can take advantage of the experience, thereby extending the positive impact. Finding a Free service or a program that the school is willing to pick up the bill for is important. Also, try choosing a company that is large enough that it just won't disappear in a couple of years.
- Using programs that are familiar especially for younger students is crucial. Students can then rely on the background knowledge of common interfaces when learning a new program, thereby reducing the time and effort needed to teach.
- Overall, a few good choice programs should be chosen in a year to concentrate on. Allowing students to have multiple attempts to refine their skills in its use. Preferably common grade level programs.

I almost never include a specific name of programs in my lesson plans as they change so often, but here is a list of programs and the function they serve. many of these programs may already be unavailable, but if not they have proven to be useful in elementary classrooms.

Paint Programs
- Tux Paint (Free) (PC/Mac)
- Doozla (Mac)

Mind Mapping
- Freeplane (Free)(PC/Mac)
- Text2MindMap.com (Free)(PC/Mac)

Word Processor
- Open Office (Free)(PC/Mac)

Keyboarding
- Tux Typing (Free)(PC/Mac)
- A Type Trainer 4 Mac (Free)(Mac)

Web Sites
- Google Sites (Free)(PC/Mac)

Apps vs. Applications (Programs)
With the influx of tablets, iPads/Android/BeOS, many schools now have the option to purchase programs that have a more targeted scope of functionality. This typically comes with a price savings which in turn can free up funds to purchase even more programs. Apps have free versions that have limited functionality, but allow teachers to preview the software before making a purchase decision. This is a perfect strategy when trying to find a program to fill the needs of the classroom.

Open Source / Free Software
Educators should be using open source or free software whenever possible. This does not mean that we should

never pay for an application, but there are many great open source programs readily available for teachers to use. There is an important reason for using open source program which is that students can download and continue using it at home as an extension to what is being learned in the classroom or to explore on their own.

Systems Configuration

Prior to the beginning of the school year, have all the computers configured for student use. As new software or hardware is introduced it will be necessary to reconfigure systems. Keep track of changes in a file to help remind those configuring the systems as to what needs to be done. This will save a lot of time and trouble.

Student Systems

The systems used by students should have three accounts configured for use before students take possession. The first account should be an administrative account, that is only used by school technicians to configure system settings. The second account should be for parents only. It is an account that has administrative permissions allowing the parent to investigate or troubleshoot system problems or issues that may arise and no other help is available. The final account to be created is for the student to use. This account should not have administrative permission, otherwise they can potentially corrupt the system.

A method that works well is to have a digital copy of the pre-configured systems stored on the network file server. Symantec has a few products that makes configuring multiple systems a breeze over the network. Another option is to have the configurations stored on a portable hard drive. This is not a good option if you re-configure all the systems over the summer as it is very time consuming.

When configuring the system, try to keep in mind how you want the user interface to look. For example, try removing shortcuts or icons to programs that are not used, or adding them to the desktop for easy access. This will eliminate confusion on the part of the student during instruction.

Teaching Tips

Working by oneself in the lab with a class full of students can be time consuming if multiple children need assistance. If this happens, it is a warning that your directions were not clear, or something unexpected happened.

Classroom Posters
Create posters with classroom rules and often used web site addresses. Place them strategically in your lab to help remind students what to do. This is a big time saver and behavior management time saver allowing you to concentrate on more important issue in your classroom.

Project Checklists
Many students are intimidated or just lose track of their progress during larger scale projects. Printing out a checklist of steps will help them manage their work. Also, include tips, but keep the checklist short and simple as to not confuse them.

Best Guess Spelling
The technology teacher shouldn't be spending time teaching children how to spell common grade level words. If students need assistance with spelling, tell them to use their best guess.

Printing
To conserve ink or toner, have students use a white background for drawings. Have them instead draw additional items to make their backgrounds interesting such as a sun or clouds.

Classroom Topics

When in doubt of a topic to use, try using a current event or ask students about what they are learning in class. These topics will be more meaningful and maintain the interest of the students.

Crazy Fonts

The bane of any teacher is when one forgets to give clear instruction as to the font and size of text. Children love to find the craziest font and often choose an inappropriate size. Have clear expectations and demonstrate to ensure that students what is expected.

Student Checklist

For typing practice, make a checklist sheet for students to keep at their station. This helps them know where they are at, so you don't have to remind them. Also, it helps the teacher know who's absent, especially at the beginning of the year when teachers are still getting to know them.

Cheat Sheets

Making a cheat sheets or posting student friendly summaries is important so students can refer back to the main ideas or points of each lesson taught.

User Accounts

Before the year begins it is important to have user accounts set up so students are ready to go once school starts. Have the IT department create individual accounts for 3-12 grade students. The accounts should be named in the manner of [year of graduation]+[first and last initial]+[unique number], for example John Doe who graduates in 2011 would be 11JD01. FI there are two people with the same initials in the same grade, the second person would be 11JD02. The account need to be roaming so students can use any computer on campus.

For the younger students, have the IT department create roaming accounts but only for the class name such as 2A or 1C. The accounts for the younger students don't need to be specific yet as having them remember passwords can be problematic. Also the younger students don't need as much network access.

Online Accounts

Have students use their school ID's and passwords when creating online accounts. This will cut down on confusion when students forget their login information, when using a program they don't use often.

Classrooms

This year all 1st and 2nd grade classes will have a blocked technology time in the computer lab located in the Elementary building. Please stop by in the morning or after school to see the lab or to ask questions about the technology curriculum.

Bulletin Board

Current student work is displayed on the bulletin board outside the computer lab. Parents and other teachers are encouraged to view work done, to help motivate students to do their best work. This is often referred to as creating an internal motivation.

Strategies for Block and Flex Classes

Block classes are run with a standard scope and sequence to ensure that all students have a solid foundation of basic skills. The basic skills are used in the computer lab by the technology teacher and the homeroom teachers. Have a set of technology skills helps all projects especially those from the homeroom run much smoother and with less interruption.

The strategy for flex classes involves helping the homeroom teacher with projects in the classroom. Keeping in touch with what is happening in the classroom helps both the homeroom and the technology teacher know what content is being taught and from the perspective of the homeroom teacher of what skills can be expected from the students. Dropping in to the homeroom classes unannounced to quietly and quickly see what is happening in the classrooms can help the technology teacher think of ways of incorporating technology with the homeroom teacher. Also, it gives insight into possible solutions to common problems within the homeroom in regards to technology.

First Grade Year Overview

1st Quarter Structured Lessons
All lessons are structured to the point where students always have clear objectives. All classroom time is utilized to teach skills, content, or both. There will never be a time when students are allowed to freely play on the computers. Even when projects are completed, students will be encouraged to elaborate or reflect on the work.

Getting to Know Your Students
The first day of class is where the student and teacher learn about each other. Learning the names of each students can be a daunting task especially in a big school. Using the first day to play a name game or getting to know you activity is important even though it may not be tied directly to the curriculum.

Classroom Etiquette & Basic Operation
The first few weeks of computer class focuses on proper classroom etiquette. The behavior of students in the computer lab should be similar to that of the library. This allows students to concentrate on their work. Also, it ensures that the computer equipment in the lab does not get damaged.

Once students understand what is expected in the lab, they learn about the basic operations of a computer. These skills include such skills as logging into their accounts and starting programs.

Starting & Stopping Programs
It is important that students learn how to start and stop programs. Once they learn this basic skill, teachers won't have to waste precious time running around helping students with a skill that should be common knowledge.

Have students start the year off by starting and stopping a basic paint program. This also helps with managing the classroom in the first few days as students are highly motivated to draw freely while you help those students who need additional help.

Hand Eye Coordination
Students need to practice basic hand eye coordination in regards to using a mouse and keyboard. Having students perform a pre-assessment that is game-like, is a great way for a teacher to judge the abilities of students before any projects commence. If a particular class or grade level is determined to be lacking in regards to hand-eye coordination, more time can be allotted to help bring their abilities up to par.

Keyboarding in the 1st Grade

The first grade classes will be learning how to type using the online typing program <u>Dance Mat Typing</u>. This program was created by the BBC and is a great way to teach children to type while keeping their interest. You can even have them practice at home and they'll think it's fun!

Voice Recording
Recording one's voice is a perfect way to get students to practice speaking in their second language. This term we are introducing the basic skills needed to successfully record their voice. Some of these skills include vocalization, understand how to record in small segments, and how to reduce background noise while recording. Even at an early age, students are able to comprehend and create great recordings that can be integrated into homeroom projects.

2nd Quarter
Basic Operations
Even though 2nd quarter is focused on the CyberSMART curriculum, also through differentiated practice students still get a chance to work on the typing skills. The program used is Tux Typing or Dance Mat Typing which are free open source or free web based programs. These are good choices as they have themes that are kid friendly and the lessons can easily be tailored to the curriculum taught in the classroom. This helps reinforce commonly used vocabulary.

Presentation Software
A major component of any technology program is to teach students how to communicate using digital tools. One of the most important applications for doing so is presentation software, such as Keynote, Comic Life, Powerpoint, or Google Presentation to name a few. Presentation software is one of the main programs used since it is versatile enough to fit into many projects. Teaching students to use it early on helps streamline projects done in collaboration with homeroom teachers. Presentation software is perfect for projects where school-wide social issues are the main focus of the project, such as bullying or fire drills as two example projects.

Storyboard Software
Students will learn how to utilize storyboard software such as Comic Life to illustrate and organize their thoughts. This is a perfect tool to use with the 6 +1 Writing Traits.

CyberSMART
The CyberSMART curriculum, which involves teaching students as well as parents how to keep their children safe in cyberspace, proper researching skills, and 21st century skills.

3rd & 4th Quarters
Basic Fact Finding Research Skills
Students in the 1st grade have learned about what a fact is and how to collect information. Also, they have learned how to note the web site used, which is a precursor to citation.

Mind-mapping

Multimedia Project
Students will learn how to piece together a multimedia presentation using Microsoft PhotoStory on the PC or iMovie using a Mac, in combination with Open Office Writer, Pages for Ma,c and Tux Paint or Doozla. This is a multifaceted project spanning multiple class sessions. First they create images of what they have learned throughout the year. Next they write a description of their pictures. Then they dictate their writing and the teacher helps piece the final presentation together for them.

Internet Safety Extension
The 2nd grade have been learning about how to stay safe online, and how to create a safe online presence, as well as basic 21st Century skills to help in learning.

Cumulative Project
Tying together all the skills and knowledge of programs used throughout the year, students create a comic using mind mapping software, word processor, image program, and a comic book page creator program. The project is broken down into stages and since this is the second time that students have used each of the individual programs, they are somewhat self-reliant. It is important to have students use each of the programs at least three times throughout the year. The first time is a demonstration, the second time the should have a solid hand holding experience, and the final third time they should create something using the skills and knowledge they have gained from the two previous lessons.

Second Grade Year Overview

1st Quarter
Structured Lessons
All lessons are structured to the point where students always have clear objectives. All classroom time is utilized to teach skills, content, or both. There will never be a time when students are allowed to freely play on the computers. Even when projects are completed, students will be encouraged to elaborate or reflect on the work.

Getting to Know Your Students
The first day of class is where the student and teacher learn about each other. Learning the names of each students can be a daunting task especially in a big school. Using the first day to play a name game or getting to know you activity is important even though it may not br tied directly to the curriculum.

Classroom Etiquette & Basic Operation
The first few weeks of computer class focuses on proper classroom etiquette. The behavior of students in the computer lab should be similar to that of the library. This allows students to concentrate on their work. Also, it ensures that the computer equipment in the lab does not get damaged.

Once students understand what is expected in the lab, they learn about the basic operations of a computer. These skills include such skills as logging into their accounts and starting programs.

Starting & Stopping Programs
It is important that students learn how to start and stop programs. Once they learn this basic skill, teachers won't have to waste precious time running around helping students with a skill that should be common knowledge.

Have students start the year off by starting and stopping a basic paint program. This also helps with managing the classroom in the first few days as students are highly motivated to draw freely while you help those students who need additional help.

Hand Eye Coordination
Students need to practice basic hand eye coordination in regards to using a mouse and keyboard. Having students perform a pre-assessment that is game-like, is a great way for a teacher to judge the abilities of students before any projects commence. If a particular class or grade level is determined to be lacking in regards to hand-eye coordination, more time can be allotted to help bring their abilities up to par.

Keyboarding in the 2nd Grade
The second grade classes will be learning how to type using the online typing program Dance Mat Typing. This program was created by the BBC and is a great way to teach children to type while keeping their interest. You can even have them practice at home and they'll think it's fun!

Voice Recording

Recording one's voice is a perfect way to get students to practice speaking in their second language. This term we are introducing the basic skills needed to successfully record their voice. Some of these skills include vocalization, understand how to record in small segments, and how to reduce background noise while recording. Even at an early age, students are able to comprehend and create great recordings that can be integrated into homeroom projects. In addition they have learned how to independently create a drawing on a particular topic to use as a storyboard for their recording prompt. Later in the year, they will use storyboards, mind maps, and written documents as their prompts.

2nd Quarter

Basic Operations

Even though 2nd quarter is focused on the CyberSMART curriculum, also through differentiated practice students still get a chance to work on the typing skills. The program used is Tux Typing or Dance Mat Typing which are free open source or free web based programs. These are good choices as they have themes that are kid friendly and the lessons can easily be tailored to the curriculum taught in the classroom. This helps reinforce commonly used vocabulary.

Presentation Software

A major component of any technology program is to teach students how to communicate using digital tools. One of the most important applications for doing so is presentation software, such as Keynote, Powerpoint, or Google Presentation to name a few. Presentation software is one of the main programs used since it is versatile enough to fit into many projects. Teaching students to use it early on helps streamline projects done in collaboration with homeroom teachers.

CyberSMART

The CyberSMART curriculum, which involves teaching students as well as parents how to keep their children safe in cyberspace, proper researching skills, and 21st century skills.

3rd & 4th Quarters

Google Maps

Mind-mapping

Basic Fact Finding Research Skills

Students in the 2nd grade have learned about what a fact is and how to collect information. Also, they have learned how to note the web site used, which is a precursor to citation.

Multimedia Project

Students will learn how to piece together a multimedia presentation using Microsoft PhotoStory on the PC or iMovie using a Mac, in combination with Openoffice Writer, Pages for Mac, and Tux Paint or Doozla. This is a multifaceted project spanning multiple class sessions. First they create images of what they have learned throughout the year. Next they write a description of their pictures. Then they dictate their writing and the teacher helps piece the final presentation together for them.

Internet Safety Extension

The 2nd grade have been learning about how to stay safe online, as well as basic 21st Century skills to help in learning.

Third, Fourth, & Fifth Grade Year Overview

iMovie or Movie Maker

Many of the 3rd grade classes are using iMovie to create commercials. This project is based on persuasive writing techniques coupled with using a storyboard which is sequencing in the 6+1 writing traits.

Internet Research Skills

The fourth grade classes are preparing students for Internet based research, by teaching basic research skills pertaining to the Internet. These skills are important and help prepare students for all aspects of using technology in the classroom.

Podcasts
Students in the fourth grade have been using Podcasts to reflect on the science projects.

Stop Frame Animation
Creating stop frame animations is a great way to explain a sequence.

Online Safety
Having students learn how to keep their identities private is a concern for many parents. Identity theft is one of the biggest problems facing people as criminals garner information from unsuspecting people using the Internet. Training people before the theft happens is better than trying to sort out an identity theft problem after the fact.

Voicethread
The fifth grade classes are using Voice Threads to work collaboratively online. Voicethread is a perfect way for students to peer review. Also, it re-enforces speaking skills taught in class.

Kindergarten Year Overview

1st Quarter
Structured Lessons
All lessons are structured to the point where students always have clear objectives. All classroom time is utilized to teach skills, content, or both. There will never be a time when students are allowed to freely play on the computers. Even when projects are completed, students will be encouraged to elaborate or reflect on the work. An exception is made for Kindergarten, where storytime is at the midpoint of every session to allow students to re-focus, and to introduce subject matter that will be used.

Getting to Know Your Students
The first day of class is where the student and teacher learn about each other. Learning the names of each students can be a daunting task especially in a big school. Using the first day to play a name game or getting to know you activity is important even though it may not be tied directly to the curriculum.

Classroom Etiquette & Basic Operation
The first few weeks of computer class focuses on proper classroom etiquette. The behavior of students in the computer lab should be similar to that of the library. This allows students to concentrate on their work. Also, it ensures that the computer equipment in the lab does not get damaged.

Once students understand what is expected in the lab, they learn about the basic operations of a computer. These skills include such skills as logging off and on, mouse control, and keyboard familiarization. The skills learned during the first part of the year are necessary in order to move the students forward into more creative endeavors later in the year. With a solid basic skill set, teachers can also take advantage of technology related projects in their classrooms. The typing and painting programs used during the year might include Tux Typing and Tux Paint for the PC, or Doozla and Dance Mat Typing for the Mac. All of which are open source or free to use programs that are available on the Internet. The goal is to find programs that parents can download and use at home to help foster the skills their children learned at school.

Due to the short focus time of the younger students, a good strategy to use is to break up the instruction time by reading a good picture book. This is a great way to incorporate a theme into the daily lesson.

Mouse Skills

It is important for the younger students to spend a good deal of time practicing their hand-eye coordination using a mouse. Having them use a paint program is a captivating way to do this while maintaining a high level of enthusiasm on the part of the student.

An example of differentiation is by using a paint program also allows students with low hand-eye coordination to make up time and practice, while the students with better mouse skills can create more elaborate drawings.

Learning to finish a project in a specified amount of time is hard for anyone to accomplish. Teaching this skill can be done using a paint program. Show students how they can use an erasure or how to start over. Let them practice these new skill, but also use the time in class to explain to them strategies to finish their work before class is over. Giving them a limit of how many times they can start over or by telling them to use their mistakes to enhance their drawings. Having an art teacher come in to demonstrate is a way in which you can turn this teachable moment into a collaborative project.

Hand Eye Coordination
Students need to practice basic hand eye coordination in regards to using a mouse and keyboard. Having students perform a pre-assessment that is game-like, is a great way for a teacher to judge the abilities of students before any projects commence. If a particular class or grade level is determined to be lacking in regards to hand-eye coordination, more time can be allotted to help bring their abilities up to par.

Basic Mouse Control Web Site
A website that is an excellent choice for younger students to learn basic mouse skills is

http://www.seniornet.org/howto/mouseexercises/mousepractice.html

Demonstrate each drill as students at an early level will not be able to read the instruction.

2nd Quarter

The second quarter students will be focusing on the CyberSMART curriculum which involves teaching students as well as parents on how to keep their children safe in cyberspace, proper researching skills, and 21st century skills.

3rd & 4th Quarters
The 3rd quarter, the technology classes should be focusing more towards collaboration with homeroom teachers. With the basic skill set no in place, students and teachers can concentrate more on creativity as opposed to basic computer skills.

Basic Mind-mapping

Typing Practice

Students even as young as kindergartners practice typing skills. Usually, it is not a main lesson, but rather a filler for short lessons or to help differentiate a lesson. Using programs such as Tux Typing or Dance Mat Typing, both of which are free to use or open source programs, they are able to learn to touch type without looking due to the visual prompts on the screen. Another great feature is the ability to create custom word lists or lessons when using Tux Typing.

Cleanliness

Communal Diseases

Sharing of equipment is a sure way to help in the spread of unwanted germs. Unfortunately many schools due to budget restraints must share devices. Practice basic cleanliness and your students will be less likely to get sick.

1. Having tissue always available.
2. Use disinfectant aerosol spray for keyboards and mice once a week.
3. Teach students how to sneeze into sleeve.
4. Remind students to not pick nose or stick fingers in their mouths.
5. Remind students to wash when leaving bathrooms.

Clubs

Throughout the Year
Working with students outside the classroom is essential in building and fostering relationships with students. Good relations with students is key in regards to respect in the classroom.

With a focus on implementing technology, we are hoping to improve athlete motivation and bringing in the parents to enjoy their child's athletic experience. Students love nothing more than to compete not only with other teams, but with themselves. Keeping statistics throughout the season enables them to compare and contrast their performance. By having a web presence for the team, we are better able to share our season with parents who often times live or work too far away.

Engineering
Basic engineering should be taught at every level in schools. The future of all modern economies is dependent on the ability to produce cutting edge innovative products.

The use of open source Arduino engineering modules make it easy for students to learn the basic concepts and to have a hands on experience. Easy to follow lessons are available online using the kits.

HTML
Using simple free programs, students can use either a PC or Mac to learn how to program using HTML to create a website on a topic of their choosing. HTML is a perfect first programming language for students to learn and a great way for students to practice and refine their logic skills. Student web sites will consist of 5 pages. An introduction page, an About page, Links page, and two Content pages solely on the topic of their choosing. Finished work will be published on the school's main website.

Lesson 1 Programs to Use
Demonstrate to students the two programs used to make a web site. The first program is Notepad. This program is used to make the web pages. The second program is IE. This is the program used to open a web page and check progress.

1. Explain what a web page is and that more than one web page make a web site.
2. Have them brainstorm a "topic" for their web site.
3. Have students get familiar with how to open programs, save and reopen a notepad document.
4. Explain what HTML is and what are "tags."
5. Have them start an Introduction page and show them basic tags, such as, HTML, BODY, P, B, and BR.

Lesson 2 Changing Simple Page Attributes
Have students open their previously saved page. Explain objects and properties. Show them how to change background color and text attributes such as font, size, and color. Hex Colors

Lesson 3 Adding Links
Have students create a links page, and add sites to it that are similar to their site.

Lesson 4 Adding Pictures
Have students go to free photo directory to gather photos for their site. Explain IMG tag. Click here to find some free photos.

Lesson 5 Image Links
Have students go to free photo directory to gather photos for their site. Explain IMG tag.

Lesson 6 Comments
Have students write comments to help them remember what they have do and would like to do.

Lesson 7 Multiple Pages
Have students create an About and Content pages.

Lesson 8 Menus
Have students create a uniform menu that can be added to their pages to help navigate their web site.

Lesson 9+ Content
Have students add content.

Innovation
The Innovation club is modeled under the Top 20 Under Twenty school. The object is to have students learn about the creative process by exploring different aspects of innovation. Students will finish the club by inventing a new product.

Requirements
- The book used throughout the term is The Ten Faces of Innovation: IDEO's Strategies for Defeating the Devil's Advocate and Driving Creativity Throughout Your Organization

Lessons
- Explore invisible items, these are everyday items that we don't take notice of, but are everywhere in our daily lives.
- Combination of invisible items, students will randomly combine objects and try and create new products.
- Exploration of invisible functions, these are actions we do everyday that we don't take notice of.
- Combination of invisible functions, combining invisible functions to create new functions.
- Combination of invisible functions and items to create new innovative products.

Final project
- Students will create a prototype of any idea that has been previously explored or come up with a new one using the techniques learned. The prototype can be in any form.
- Apply to the Top 20 Under Twenty program

Instructors Mark Page & Tim Bray

Scratch
Scratch is a graphical high level programming environment, which is easy to use especially for younger students.

Lessons Overview
- Introduction to Scratch. Students play with the block scripting components.
- Scratch basic video tutorials. Students use the simple video tutorials to explore the graphical components of Scratch.
- Learn to modify pre-existing game. Students create an account on MIT's site and download a pre-existing game and learn to modify it using the "educated experimentation" method.
- Learn to make a calculator. Students use silent video tutorials to learn about variables by making a calculator.

Core PDI Units

There are many Core units that can be developed in conjunction with staff, students, and parents. a good place to start is with ISTE's NETS standards and benchmarks. Below are listed some Core Units that might help to get a program started.

- Digital citizenship
  - Learning at all levels about the impact of technology in our everyday lives. Obvious curriculum tie in is Social Studies.
- Research
  - Learning proper researching skills and copyright. Obvious curriculum tie in is Social Studies.
- Multimedia
  - Using media to help convey content is a perfect use of technology in the classroom. Obvious curriculum tie in is all subjects.
- Social Media
  - Online tools are key in today's world. One of the strong points for social media is not only conveying a message, but for collaboration. Obvious curriculum tie in is all subjects.
- Collaborative Productivity Suite
  - Soon all productivity suites will have an online version. The strengths of the online suite such as Microsoft's SkyDrive and Google's Docs is the power of collaboration, paperless, accessibility, and cross platform. In addition they are free. Obvious curriculum tie in is all subjects.
- Devices
  - Learning about the different options of tools availability and how and when to use them are import for everyone to learn. Obvious curriculum tie in is all subjects.

Meaningful Technology Integration

Combining different technology units together with a core curriculum unit, leads to a more holistic meaningful approach to technology integration.

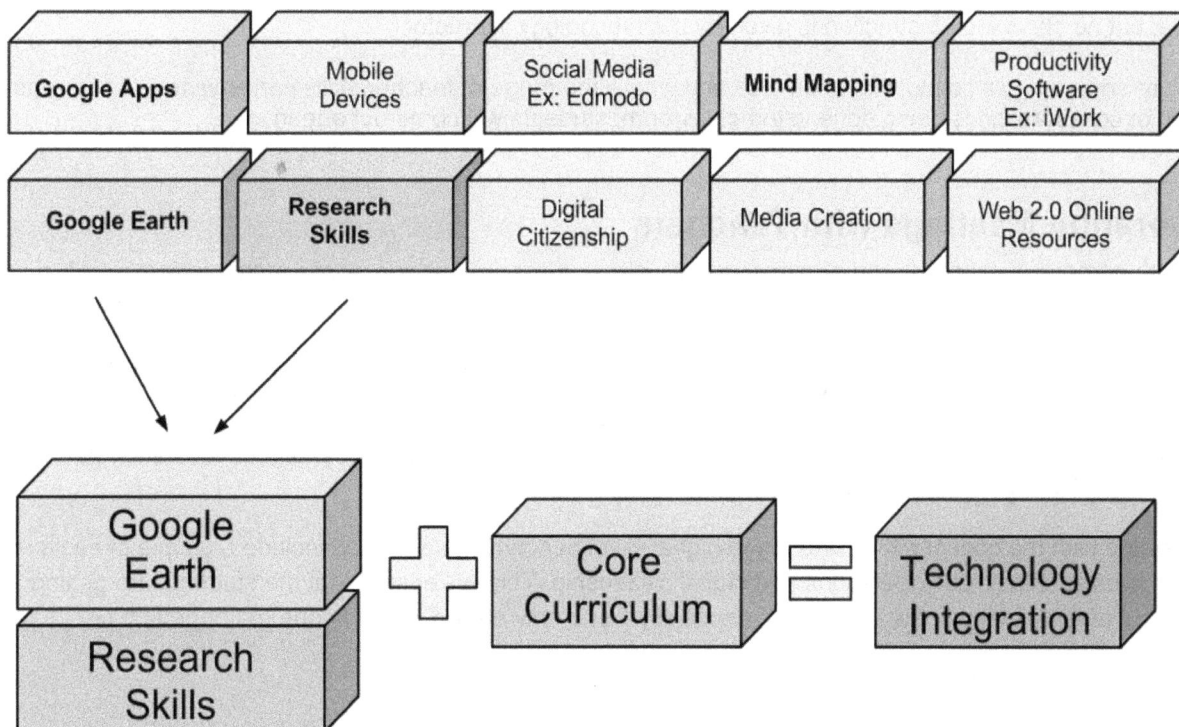

Curriculum

Mapping out the technology related skills and techniques for utilizing technology is important to map out prior to the term starting. However, with the rapidly changing world, we need to be adaptable. many factors such as new software or hardware, and even technique and usage all become potential new units in pre-existing curriculum.

Three Methods of Technology Collaboration
For the Technology Guru Teachers
Give them the strands, NETS is a good place to start, and let them come to you when they are unsure.

For the Teacher Who are Somewhat Confident
Give them the strands, NETS is a good place to start, and also give them suggestions on how to integrate technology.

For the Apprehensive Teacher
Give them the strands, NETS is a good place to start, and request openly to have their students come in or to let you teach them specific skills.

Collaboration

There are three types of collaboration that can take place in the classroom in regards to technology Direct, Cooperative, and Passive. The first is Direct collaboration. This is where the technology instructor creates and delivers instruction based on what is being taught in the classroom with little or no interaction from the homeroom teacher. This is the easiest, but not necessarily the best option, as the content can tend to be heavily based on technology. Cooperative is the ideal situation as the technology instructor and the teacher teach together the technology skills and the content interwoven in the lesson. The last option is Passive. This is a situation when the technology instructor just assists the homeroom teacher if individual students need assistance, but no class wide instruction is given by the technology instructor.

All forms are common in a school that is diverse and where the range of teacher skills varies widely. As long as some form of collaboration is being done in the classroom, students will come out ahead.

Collaboration Meetings with Teachers

Meeting with homeroom teachers and other specialists is a vital aspect to a successful technology integration program. At time teachers may request that the technology integration teacher attend a grade level meeting. Before attending such a meeting, the technology instructor should be familiar with the Technology Standards and Benchmarks. This will enable the structure of the brainstorm and planning portions of any project to take a more meaningful approach as opposed to just adding tidbits of technology to fulfill a technology requirement. Having targeted Standards and benchmarks should be the starting point. The basic operations benchmarks can be added to any projects, but implementing some of the higher order and less flashy benchmarks such as research and analysis can be the harder one to integrate.

Start a meeting with the goal of hitting one of the higher level benchmarks and then include a couple of easily achievable ones such as basic operations and digital citizenship. This will ensure that the students are getting the mostly out of technology in the classroom, especially if you only are able to fit in one major project per year.

Structure of Classroom Collaboration
Three part structure of incorporating technology in the classroom

1. Demonstration is the first step where students are introduced to the concept, software and hardware that

will be used in the project.

2. Exploration is the step where students get to use the different aspects that they have seen and instructed to use.

3. Creation is where students use the skills and concepts to create a final product following the criteria given by the homeroom teacher.

Social aspect such as responsibility should be integrated into every project. (Cyberbullying, plagiarism)

Observational assessment is the easiest type of assessment. It is easier to use because collaborative projects are time consuming and often there is not enough time to do a formal assessment of a finished product. Also, many of the technology skills are not product related, such as keyboarding as opposed to creating a printed report.

Rubrics and benchmark checklist should be given to homeroom teachers prior to lesson. Students should also be told how they will be assessed.

Elementary Continuum

	1st Quarter	2nd Quarter	3rd Quarter	4th Quarter
Kindergarten	ISTE NETS (1, 2, 5, 6) **Overview** Basic Operations and Concepts, Mouse Skills Social, Ethical, and Human Issues, Lab rules Productivity Tools, Graphics **Proper computer lab rules will be introduced and responsible care of resources. Basic mouse skills. Using Drawing Program to learn basic**	ISTE NETS (1-6) **Overview** Basic Operations and Concepts, Navigating Operating System Social, Ethical, and Human Issues, Lab rules Productivity Tools, Simple Presentations **Continued practice of basic computers skills using Drawing Program. Using graphic images and voice to create digital storytelling presentation. Main focus on CyberSMART curriculum.**	ISTE NETS (1-6) **Overview** Basic Operations and Concepts, Navigating Operating System Social, Ethical, and Human Issues, Lab rules Productivity Tools, Simple Presentations **Continued practice of basic computers skills using Drawing Program. Using graphic images and voice to create digital storytelling presentation. Main focus on CyberSMART curriculum.**	ISTE NETS (1-5) **Overview** Basic Operations and Concepts, Keyboarding, Log On/Off Social, Ethical, and Human Issues, Lab rules Productivity Tools, Simple Presentations Communications Tools, Visual/Audio Presentations (assisted) Research Tools **Homeroom Projects Mindmapping (Sorting) Continued practice of basic computers skills. Learn to log on to computer and navigate to web**

31

	hand eye coordination using input devices. Students learn how to use menus while continuing to practice their basic mouse skills.			**pages. They will learn to type using web based Typing program.**
1st Grade	ISTE NETS (1, 2, 5, 6) **Overview** Basic Operations and Concepts, Keyboarding, Log On/Off Social, Ethical, and Human Issues, Lab rules Productivity Tools, Graphics **Proper computer lab rules will be introduced and responsible care of resources. Students learn to log on and use Internet browser to locate school home page. They will learn to type using web based Typing program.**	ISTE NETS (1-6) **Overview** Basic Operations and Concepts, Keyboarding Social, Ethical, and Human Issues, Lab rules Productivity Tools, Simple Presentations and beginning Word Processing Problem Solving & Decision Making Tools, Mind Maps **Continued practice of basic computers skills. Using images made in conjunction with voice overlay to create digital presentation. Continued keyboarding practice. Main focus on CyberSMART curriculum.**	ISTE NETS (1-6) **Overview** Basic Operations and Concepts, Keyboarding Social, Ethical, and Human Issues, Lab rules Productivity Tools, Simple Presentations and beginning Word Processing Problem Solving & Decision Making Tools, Mind Maps **Continued practice of basic computers skills. Using images made in conjunction with voice overlay to create digital presentation. Continued keyboarding practice. Main focus on CyberSMART curriculum.**	ISTE NETS (1-5) **Overview** Basic Operations and Concepts, Keyboarding, Social, Ethical, and Human Issues, Lab rules Productivity Tools, Simple Presentations Technology Communications Tools, Visual/Audio Presentations (assisted) Research Tools **Homeroom Projects Mindmapping (Sorting). Continued practice of basic computers skills. Mind Mapping software will be introduced. Continued keyboarding practice.**

2nd Grade	ISTE NETS (2, 5, 6)	ISTE NETS (1-6)	ISTE NETS (1-6)	ISTE NETS (1-5)
	Overview Basic Operations and Concepts, Keyboarding, Log On/Off Social, Ethical, and Human Issues, Lab rules Productivity Tools, Graphics	**Overview** Basic Operations and Concepts, Keyboarding Social, Ethical, and Human Issues, Lab rules Productivity Tools, Portfolios Problem Solving & Decision Making Tools, Mind Maps Communications Tools, Email	**Overview** Basic Operations and Concepts, Keyboarding Social, Ethical, and Human Issues, Lab rules Productivity Tools, Portfolios Problem Solving & Decision Making Tools, Mind Maps Communications Tools, Email	**Overview** Basic Operations and Concepts, Keyboarding Social, Ethical, and Human Issues, Lab rules Productivity Tools, Keyboarding Communications Tools, Visual/Audio Presentations (assisted) Research Tools, Research Skills
	Proper computer lab rules will be introduced and responsible care of resources. Students learn to log on and use Internet browser to locate school home page. They will learn to type using web based Dance Mat Typing program.	**Continued practice of basic computers skills. Mind Mapping software will be introduced. Continued keyboarding practice. Introduction to email and network use. Portfolio project using presentation software. Main focus on CyberSMART curriculum.**	**Continued practice of basic computers skills. Mind Mapping software will be introduced. Continued keyboarding practice. Introduction to email and network use. Portfolio project using presentation software. Main focus on CyberSMART curriculum.**	**Homeroom Projects Mind Mapping (Maps) Transition to Grade 3 - Desktops > Laptops - Tech Use Expectations - Computer Lab > Mobile Carts - Possibly Grade 3 students join class for peer teaching** **Continued practice of basic computers skills. Continued use of presentation software. Wiki introduction. Continued keyboarding practice.**

Core Units Scaffolding

Zone of Proximal Development Considerations

In order to keep the standards and benchmarks easily understandable and easy to use, the mention of hardware and software is intentionally left non-specific. This is to help ensure the longevity which in turn keeps a more consistent feel and lessens the need for additional time for training. In addition, there is no grouping or differentiating by grade level. In theory all standards and benchmarks can be achieved regardless of age. There are some techniques and special considerations to help each grade level achieve the successful application of each of the benchmarks.

Any software platform, ecosystem, or device manufacturer can be used to achieve goals based on NETS. Keeping the descriptions generic ensures that we as teachers are concentrating our units and efforts based on generic skills that are transferable to any system regardless of its brand name. Our goal is to aim for a student that can adapt their skill set regardless to whatever situation they may find themselves in. This is especially important in regards to technology, which changes at an incredibly rapid pace.

Pre-K - Grade 2

Teacher assistance will be important in this age group. All online resources should be carefully screened beforehand to ensure content and age level appropriateness. Individual social skills should be heavily focused on with this age group.

Grades 3-5

Students should be introduced and start using collaborative online programs by this stage for a good deal of their work. Basic research skills should also be focused on. Re-enforcing individual social skills should start to give way to a more group focused awareness.

Middle School

For simplicity of instruction, students should use one type of operating system and platform, but instruction should be non-specific so skills can be easily transferred at a later time. Collaborative online programs should be highlighted. A move to a paperless classroom model should be an important target for this age group. Their awareness of the impact they have on the digital world around them, in particular their friend groups, should be a major focus.

High School

More advanced programs can be used, especially using multiple devices and applications within projects to utilize higher level thinking. Concentration on professional level programs should be focused on. Multiple platforms should be explored as students may encounter any type of system once in the real world work environment. All work should be paperless.

Creativity and Innovation

Students demonstrate creative thinking, construct knowledge, and develop innovative products and processes using technology.

Apply existing knowledge to generate new ideas, products, or processes

The purpose of this benchmark is to have students to take their background knowledge and to create something new, be it a new idea, product, or way of using or doing something. A key point is that technology can be used but doesn't have to be the actual end product.
- **Use pre-existing knowledge to produce a document either print or digital**

Create original works as a means of personal or group expression

Having students create something in a group environment or individually can be either a print or digital work. In addition the tools used don't necessarily need to be collaborative themselves, as working together in the presence of others as long as they use technology can be considered collaborative.

- **Without using existing information produce a document either print or digital** Office suites, graphic programs, presentation programs, multimedia creation programs

Use models and simulations to explore complex systems and issues

There are many programs both online and workstation based that can be used to do labs, or model. Science labs or popular especially online, and many are free to use. In addition, there are many technology based kits that can be purchased that offer a multitude of exploration opportunities.

- **Programming using equations or functions to test**
- **Use robotics to test**
- **Lab simulation programs**

Identify trends and forecast possibilities

Keeping track of data and looking for patterns can be done in many ways. For younger students using software to identify patterns in a graphic organizer, to older students reflecting on the identification of trends found in social media.

- **Use Spreadsheets to create graphs to look for patterns**
- **Use Social Media to look for trends**

Communication and Collaboration

Students use digital media and environments to communicate and work collaboratively, including remotely, to support individual learning and contribute to the learning of others.

Interact, collaborate, and publish with peers, experts, or others employing a variety of digital environments and media

With the proliferation of online collaborative tools, finding an application to use should be easy. Many schools already use such tools and students might already have access to them. In addition, there are many online social sites that can be used. For younger students, there are many sand box social environments that teachers can use.

- **Cloud Based Tools** Online collaborative office suites
- **Use basic communication tools such as printing out a flyer or using email**
- **Use static or dynamic web sites to publish a message or content.**
- **Use social media to share information.**

Communicate information and ideas effectively to multiple audiences using a variety of media and formats

Teaching students about the different methods of communication is important. For younger students communicating using technology can be as simple as producing an image using a drawing program and posting it on the classroom wall. Older students can go as far as to publish using real-world projects to news agencies, or school based publications.

- **Basic communication tools** Teacher Led
- **Social Media (closed environment)**
- **Social Media**

Develop cultural understanding and global awareness by engaging with learners of other cultures

Using collaborative tools and/or social media to work with other students in different regions is now easily achieved. The idea of a flat-classroom, or classrooms without walls is a popular and achievable goal today.

- **Social Media Learning Community** Teacher led online discussion or message threads, Wiki, Edmodo
- **Communication Programs** Voice/Video over IP (Skype, Google Hangouts)

Contribute to project teams to produce original works or solve problems

Many online collaborative solutions exist, but in addition media creation offline can also achieve the same goal. A movie, presentation, of publication of print material if done in a group setting with specific roles for the team members offline is a simple and easy solution. Using technology to keep track of roles and work schedules, or timelines.

- **Online Multimedia Programs** VoiceThread, Glogster, Google Apps.

Research and Information Fluency

Students apply digital tools to gather, evaluate, and use information.

Plan strategies to guide inquiry

Brainstorming software or graphic organizers can be used to plan projects or be part of the process.

- **concept maps or graphic organizers**

Locate, organize, analyze, evaluate, synthesize, and ethically use information from a variety of sources and media

Finding information using a variety of resources can start from early years and lead into more unconventional places to find information such as social media sites. For more advanced students, learning database fundamentals and citation are important aspects to understanding of data and how it is organized.

- **Alpha Indexes & Link Farms**
- **Directories & Search Engines**
- **Search Features including advanced search features**
- **Social Media Sources**

Evaluate and select information sources and digital tools based on the appropriateness to specific tasks

Teaching students about who is posting information and the purpose for the propagation or dissemination of information is a critical skill. Reflection is an important process in the understanding of the validity of information found in both print and online information. Researching skills can play an important part in the validating of all information.

- **Use of digital sources such as search directories, link farms, and search engines.**
- **Understanding Audience and Purpose**

Process data and report results

Finding and processing of data can be done using an variety of tools, from graphic organizers to spreadsheets. Spreadsheets and graphing programs are useful and so is scripting, which is a more simplistic means of programming. For the reporting of results, publishing a simple print document to creating a collaborative web site such as a wiki or blog can suffice.

- **Online Presence**
- **Spreadsheets**
- **Concept maps or graphic organizers**

Critical Thinking, Problem Solving, and Decision Making

Students use critical thinking skills to plan and conduct research, manage projects, solve problems, and make informed decisions using appropriate digital tools and resources.

Identify and define authentic problems and significant questions for investigation

Finding trends in social media can be used to find topics for investigation. Also, polling an audience is a resource that can be used at any grade level.
- **Use of polling application or function**
- **concept maps or graphic organizers**

Plan and manage activities to develop a solution or complete a project

Using online collaborative sites can help students manage projects. The use shared locations on networks or on the Internet can help facilitate projects.
- **Mind Maps**
- **Shared resource location**
- **Collaborative office suite**

Collect and analyze data to identify solutions and/or make informed decisions

Using spreadsheets to collect and analyze data can be done collaboratively or individually.
- **multimedia programs**

Use multiple processes and diverse perspectives to explore alternative solutions

The key to diverse perspectives is to gain information from multiple locations. For more advanced students reaching out to other groups using online tools can be helpful. For younger students having teachers facilitate the online or polling of individuals is a good place to start. Research using print and online sources can also fulfill the diverse perspectives as well.
- **Combination of collecting information from multiple places, such as online, print, and polling culminating in a reflection and citing of sources.**

Digital Citizenship

Students understand human, cultural, and societal issues related to technology and practice legal and ethical behavior.

Advocate and practice safe, legal, and responsible use of information and technology

Having students create publications on the responsible use of technology for younger students, and having older students use proper citation and paraphrasing.
- **Safety & Security Online**
- **Manners, Cyberbullying, & Ethics**

Exhibit a positive attitude toward using technology that supports collaboration, learning, and productivity

Students tend to enjoy playing online multi-player educational games with their classmates and others online. For older students having them work collaboratively online demonstrates a positive attitude to working with others.
- **multi-player games**

- online office suite projects

Demonstrate personal responsibility for lifelong learning

Having all students participate in a technology expectations lesson a couple of times a year with projects based on appropriate use demonstrates lifelong learning and respect towards the use of technology.
- **Technology Use Expectations**

Exhibit leadership for digital citizenship

Have students use technology in a collaborative environment, or practicing safe and legal use demonstrates appropriate participation.
- **Model and collaborate using technology**

Technology Operations and Concepts

Students demonstrate a sound understanding of technology concepts, systems, and operations.

Select and use applications effectively and productively

Have students discuss or reflect on what technology tools or skill would be used to accomplish a problem.
- **Students choose to use software, or equipment**

Troubleshoot systems and applications

Let students demonstrate their ability to use a new aspect of technology. Problem solving in a group could also help demonstrator if reflection is part of the lesson.
- **Learn to use new hardware or software. Can also include using technology in a new way.**

Transfer current knowledge to learning of new technologies

Using similar aspects of technology is a common thread that needs to be re-enforced. For example all ecosystems keep a similar user interface that when presented to student can demonstrate their understanding and whether they are able to adapt their background knowledge.
- **Ability to use a similar system**

Understand and use technology systems

The basic operations of technology includes understanding of basic common aspects of systems, user input devices, and more deeply for older students the intuition of where to look to find functions of devices when presented with a new device environment.
- **Beginning Skills**
- **Keyboarding**
- **Mobile Devices**
- **Input Devices**
- **Network Architecture**

CyberSMART

What is CyberSMART?

Common Sense Media has coordinated with the free CyberSmart curriculum to create an integrated K-12 Digital Literacy and Citizenship curriculum.

Reference: http://cybersmartcurriculum.org

Motivation (Personal Observations)
- Family (safety & identity theft)
- Lack of Direction in Field (research)
- Continuous Putting Out of Fires (both)

Why We Need It:
Safety, http://www.youtube.com/watch?v=_o8auwnJtqE
Social Blunders, http://cnettv.cnet.com/personal-digital-disasters/9742-1_53-50102663.html

Immediate Concerns
Is there an Impact in Learning?
- Lost-time due to Experimentation
- Bells & Whistles

Social Media (safety)
- What was Said, can't take back
- Bullying (facts)
- Forgetfulness of Surroundings

Digital Native Myth (Jamie McKenzie) (research)
- Research
- Communication
- Citizenship

Role of Educators

- Assume Parents are busy
- Assume Teachers are busy
- Teachers "can be" 1st line of defense (safety)
- Ensure minimum skill set (Research)

CyberSMART What is it?

K-12 Digital Literacy & Citizenship Curriculum
Both Research & Safety focused
Standards-based
Prepares students communication, creativity, collaboration, critical thinking, and problem solving

Benefits
- Preparation for Web 2.0
- No reinvention
- Aligned K-12
- ISTE's NETS integration
- Pre-made lesson plans
- Home Connection
- Piecemeal-able

- FREE

SMART

S = Safety and Security Online
M = Manners & Cyber Citizenship
A = Authentic Learning and Creativity
R = Research and Information Fluency
T = Twenty-First Century Challenges

Safety & Security Online

Strategies for fostering online safety, privacy, and security in support of student learning

- Identity theft, personal safety, and privacy
- Cyberbullying, pornography, and disruptive student Web sites
- Filters and computer security
- At-risk student warning signals and efficacy of scare tactics
- Social networking and online collaboration and communication

Manners, Bullying, & Ethics

Strategies for fostering academic integrity, addressing social and ethical concerns, and encouraging responsible digital citizenship

- Plagiarism
- Hate sites, cyberbullying, and inappropriate content
- Citations, sources, copyright, and fair use
- Character development

Authentic Learning and Creativity

Hands-on practice in using the Internet to facilitate higher-order thinking skills—moving beyond copy-and-paste assignments

- Critical thinking
- Essential questions to drive learning
- Inquiry skills and authentic problem-based learning
- Web 2.0 tools to stimulate thinking
- Inquiry-based learning and social constructivist strategy

Research and Information Fluency

Online search skills to support information fluency and student learning

- Locating and evaluating online resources
- Search terms and advanced search techniques
- Subject directories, subscription databases, the "invisible web," and primary sources
- How school libraries impact student test score

Twenty-First Century Challenge

The implications of a digitally connected world for instructional strategies, and using the Internet to support the diverse needs of learners.

- Millennial learning styles
- Digital equity and assistive technologies for at-risk and underserved populations
- The changing roles of librarians, teachers, and administrators

Tips & Tricks

- Send home Home Connection & Post Bulletin Board
- Have workspace for non-electronic work
- Create Rubric
- Create Score Sheet

Assessment

- Linked to NETS
- Uses scoring rubric -» Link to benchmarks
- Send immediate feedback (best practice)
- Keep parents informed using Home Connection

Pros

- Free
- Scoped and sequenced
- Pre-made lesson plans K-12
- Use as a framework

Cons

- Limited amount of lessons (some categories)
- Time, some lessons 45 minutes +
- Early grades have less lessons
- Some lessons may not be leveled for your school.

Other Great Cyber Safety Programs

- NetSmartz.org
- KidsHealth.org
- iKeepSafe.org
- ThinkuKnow.co.uk

Differentiating

Differentiating Instruction

- Pre-test to assess student ability.
- Develop and foster intrinsic motivation
- Instill a sense of fairness

Four Ways to Differentiate Instruction:

1. **Content/Topic:** skip the instruction step (compacting the curriculum), permit the apt student to accelerate their rate of progress
2. **Process/Activities:** alternative paths to manipulate the ideas embedded within the concept. For example graphic organizers, maps, diagrams or charts, Varying the complexity

3. **Product:** varying the complexity of the product, reduced / increase performance expectations
4. **Environment or Learning Styles:** Blended Multiple Intelligences teaching style (visual mind mapping, kinesthetic acting)

The Strategies:

- Readiness / Ability
- Visual Clues
- Adjusting Questions (Bloom's taxonomy)
- Compacting Curriculum
- Tiered Assignments
- Acceleration/Deceleration Pace
- Flexible Grouping
- Buddy Instruction Discussion
- Independent Study Projects
- Group Projects
- Learning Centres

* Source http://www.members.shaw.ca/priscillatheroux/differentiatingstrategies.html

Emergency Lesson Plan

Always have an emergency lesson plan ready. Have students practice skill sets that they may need help on or can improve on.

Emergency Lesson Plan Technology Grades One & Two

Escort the students into class once they are quietly waiting in line at the door. I maintain a strict Library quiet atmosphere in the room at all times. Students know this!

Overview

Once students are seated on the carpet, explain that they will be practicing their typing skills and when done, they will create a drawing using Doozla with at least 3 colors and 3 different pens. They must also label, add a title, and put their names on their drawings. Students are not allowed to just scribble or draw non-topic drawings. You can pick a topic of what they are to draw.

Body of Lesson

Students have assigned seating. They are not allowed out of their seats once seated. Call out their names one by one and hand them their typing slip, which are located in my desk. They are not allowed to handle the slips at any time other than when sitting down at the beginning of the period. Each slip contains the computer number, you will need to collect the slips after class.

Each student is to work on next lesson as stated on their personal typing slip. If no slip is found for student, or if they are done with the lessons, they can play Tux Typing. They are to do medium to hard levels and must do a word list, not the "alphabet" lesson. Monitor student progress. Do NOT check off students on their typing slips. If questioned by the student, tell them that today is for practice only. Once they finish their typing lesson or once you reach the midpoint of the class period, have them start Doozla and create their drawing of whatever subject matter you like.

With a few minutes to spare before the end of class, announce aloud "Log-out!" Students will log-out, straighten their workstations, push-in their chairs, and quietly stand behind their chairs. When the homeroom teacher or aide comes, students will quietly walk single file out of the room.

Grades 3-5 Lessons

Technology Lessons for Grades 3-5

Here are lessons used in collaboration with grades 3-5 teachers and specialists. They are ordered by the six different ISTE's NETS strands, and can be taught in any order as needed. All lessons can be taught in the lab or using the carts. Teachers need not be present. This page will be updated as new lessons are added.

Assessments are optional, but can done using the general grading rubric (see below) if requested.

Basic Operations / Beginning of the Year Lessons
- <u>Computer Expectations</u> (~20-30 minutes), **Objective:** This lesson is basically a lecture on the yearlong expectations for using technology at school. **Assessment Suggestion:** Written or oral reflection. **ISTE NETS Strand: Digital Citizenship.**
- <u>Typing Pre/Mid/Post-Assessment</u> (~10 minutes), Objective: A typing assessment is needed to figure out which students need help in order to catch up with the rest of the class. Having all students within an acceptable pace for typing allows teachers to teach content in a timely manner. Assessment Suggestion: N/A. ISTE NETS Strand: **Technology Operations and Concepts**
- <u>Keyboarding Introduction</u> (~20-30 minutes), **Objective:** After assessment a basic introduction to keyboarding skills should be given to ensure that students have a clear understanding on what to do and what is expected. **Assessment Suggestion:** Online timed typing test. **ISTE NETS Strand: Technology Operations and Concepts**
- <u>Basic Account Login and Setup</u> (~30 minutes), **Objective:** Students will need to learn the basics about logging in and how to navigate the Operating System and common programs that they will use at the beginning of the year. **Assessment Suggestion:** Observational assessment. **ISTE NETS Strand: Technology Operations and Concepts**

Digital Citizenship / Internet Safety & Skills
- <u>CyberSMART</u> **Safety & Security online** (~30-45 minutes), **Objective:** Learning what information is private is key to student safety. **Assessment Suggestion:** See CyberSMART lesson details. **ISTE NETS Strand:** Multiple strands, see lesson details.
  - K-1, One lesson
  - 2-3, Two lessons
    - What's Private?
    - Filling Out a Form—Ask First
  - 4-5, Five lessons
    - Private Information
    - Safe Talking in Cyberspace
    - Powerful Passwords
    - Handling E-mail and IM
    - Privacy Rules!
- <u>CyberSMART</u> **Manners, Cyberbullying, & Ethics** (~30-45 minutes) **Objective:** Important lessons dealing with beginning citation, and how to avoid unpleasant situations in an online environment. **Assessment Suggestion:** See CyberSMART lesson details. **ISTE NETS Strand:** Multiple strands, see

lesson details.
- K-1, One lesson
- 2-3, Four lessons
  - Everyone Wants Friends
  - Is That Fair?
  - Whose Property Is This?
  - Good Manners Everywhere
- 4-5, Nine lessons
  - The Power of Words
  - Groupthink
  - Be Comfortable
  - Citizens of Cyberspace
  - Understand Your Acceptable Use Policy
  - Speak Out
  - Whose Is It, Anyway?
  - Do the Right Thing
  - Good E-mail Manners

- **CyberSMART Authentic Learning & Creativity** (~30-45 minutes) **Objective:** N/A. **Assessment Suggestion:** See CyberSMART lesson details. **ISTE NETS Strand:** Multiple strands, see lesson details.
  - K-1, N/A
  - 2-3, One lessons
    - The Power of Writing
  - 4-5, One lessons
    - Purchasing Power

- **CyberSMART Research & Information Fluency** (~30-45 minutes) **Objective:** How to use information from online sources in a proper method. **Assessment Suggestion:** See CyberSMART lesson details. **ISTE NETS Strand:** Multiple strands, see lesson details.
  - K-1, Four lessons
  - 2-3, Five lessons
    - Subject Category Searching
    - Using Keywords
    - Finding Good Sites
    - Ask a Librarian
    - Things for Sale
  - 4-5, Six lessons
    - Choosing a Search Site
    - Rating Web Sites
    - Homework Help in a Hurry
    - E-mailing for Homework Help
    - What's at the Library?
    - A Place to Advertise

- **CyberSMART 21st Century** (~30-45 minutes) **Objective:** Online collaborative tool use. **Assessment Suggestion:** See CyberSMART lesson details. **ISTE NETS Strand:** Multiple strands, see lesson details.
  - K-1, Two lessons
  - 2-3, Two lessons
    - What's the Big Idea?
    - My Cyberspace Neighborhood
  - 4-5, Four lessons
    - Great Communicators
    - Cyberspace Country
    - What Is a Network?
    - Imagining the Future

Collaboration / Online Presentation Tools

- **Voicethread** (30-40 minutes) **Objective:** Online presentation software use. **Assessment Suggestion:** Published presentation using VoiceThread. **ISTE NETS Strand:** Creativity and Innovation, Communication and Collaboration, Digital Citizenship, Technology Operations and Concepts.
- **Google Apps** (+1 hours minutes), **Objective:** This is a lesson on how to setup and start using Google Apps, an office suite similar to MS Ofiice or iWork. Introduction to Google Docs with a hands on experience with online collaboration. Chat fundamentals, commenting, and behavioral issues are also discussed. **Assessment Suggestion:** Creation of and collaboration of Google App document. **ISTE NETS Strand: Communication and Collaboration, Digital Citizenship, Technology Operations and Concepts.**
    - **Gmail (usually needs follow-up lessons)**
    - **Google Chrome (learn to use apps within Chrome browser)**
    - **Google Documents (usually needs follow-up lessons)**
    - **Google Forms**
    - **Google Groups**
    - **Google Presentation**
    - **Google Search (usually needs follow-up lessons)**
    - **Google Sites**
    - **Google Spreadsheet**
- **Google Gmail** (+1 hours minutes), **Objective:** This is a lesson on how to setup and start using Google Gmail. Gmail, including Friendly Letter format followed by creation of email. Emphasis on appropriate use. Upper grades will learn proper password creation. **Assessment Suggestion:** Email in Friendly Letter format. **ISTE NETS Strand: Communication and Collaboration, Digital Citizenship, Technology Operations and Concepts.**

Productivity & Creativity

- **Word Processor Spreadsheet, Presentation,** this can include Pages, Google Docs, Word, or Openoffice (45 minutes), **Objective:** Basic fundamentals of using a productivity document are taught allowing students to create documents. **Assessment Suggestion:** Creation of productivity document. ISTE NETS Strand: **Creativity and Innovation, Digital Citizenship, Technology Operations and Concepts.**
- **Google Earth (30-40 minutes), Objective:** Using geography to elaborate or create a meaningful project for just about every subject matter is easy and powerful when done on a globe. Google Earth allows for written narratives, as well as combined use of voice, video, or still images in conjunction with location, allowing for an in depth analysis of project material. **Assessment Suggestion:** ISTE NETS Strand: **Creativity and Innovation, Research and Information Fluency, Digital Citizenship, Technology Operations and Concepts.**
    - Lesson 1, Introduction to using Google Earth (GE) as a research tool.
    - Lesson 2, Use GE to create a file of placemarks that is sent to teacher for assessment.
    - Lesson 3, Create a Tour of places of interest that is sent to teacher for assessment.
    - Lesson 4, Create a Recording of places of interest that is sent to teacher for assessment.

Research

- **Basic research skills (30-40 minutes),** Objective: Introduction to different options for searching, and key word and phrase use, child safe searching is explained, and Advance search techniques. **Assessment Suggestion:** Collection of pertinent information, and proper citation. **ISTE NETS Strand: Research and Information Fluency, Digital Citizenship.**
    - Introduction Lesson
    - Follow-up (review) lesson

Critical Thinking

- **Mind Mapping (30-40 minutes),** Objective: Mind mapping is a tool used to help students create and organize their thoughts using a program allowing them to easily re-organize and categorize. Perfect for Pre-writing or even to be used as a research tool. **Assessment Suggestion:** Creation of mind map. **ISTE NETS Strand: Critical Thinking, Problem Solving, and Decision Making**

General Grading Rubric

Below is a general grading rubric which can be used for all projects. Most projects especially skill based projects don't always need a precise rubric. However, this rubric can be made more specific to include skills or objects that need to be addressed.

Grade	Student is unable to start or continue without direct instruction. Little to no evidence of understanding of concept(s). Takes a reclusive role in task.	Occasionally needs instruction to finish task. Evidence that student is starting to grasp concept(s). Takes an passive role in task.	Clear and easy to understand all required tasks are fulfilled. Able to convey understanding of concept(s). Takes an passive role in task.	Elaborated or added personal connections or elements that go above and beyond required task. Full understanding of concept(s) and able to elaborate. Takes an active role in task.
K-2	I don't understand and need help. I didn't asked questions and did not help others.	I need help to start or finish. I asked questions or helped others.	I can do it by myself. I helped a friend or asked questions.	I can do it by myself, and I did more than the teacher asked me to do. I helped a friend and asked questions.
3-5	I don't understand and need help throughout the project. I didn't asked questions and did not help others.	I don't understand and need help on what to do in order to finish task. I asked questions or helped others.	I can do it by myself, but may need some help. I asked questions or helped others.	I can do it by myself. I understand the concepts, and I did more than the teacher asked of me to do. I asked questions and helped others.

Integration Minimum Coverage

Below is a guide to what a minimum curriculum scope and sequencing of lesson can look like over the course of a school year. This is just a suggestion and should be modified to fill the needs of each school and their student body.

Kindergarten	Computer expectations, keyboarding pre-assessment, Digital Citizenship, Research	Keyboarding mid-assessment, Research	Keyboarding post-assessment, Research

1st Grade	Computer expectations, keyboarding pre-assessment, Digital Citizenship, Research	Keyboarding mid-assessment, Research	Keyboarding post-assessment, Research
2nd Grade	Computer expectations, keyboarding pre-assessment, Digital Citizenship, Research	Keyboarding mid-assessment, Research	Keyboarding post-assessment, Research
3rd Grade	Computer expectations, keyboarding pre-assessment, Digital Citizenship, Research	Keyboarding mid-assessment, Research	Keyboarding post-assessment, Research
4th Grade	Computer expectations, keyboarding pre-assessment, Digital Citizenship, Research	Keyboarding mid-assessment, Research	Keyboarding post-assessment, Research
5th Grade	Computer expectations, keyboarding pre-assessment, Digital Citizenship, Research	Keyboarding mid-assessment, Introduction to Google Apps, Research	Keyboarding post-assessment, Google Apps Collaboration, Research

ISTE NETS

Who is ITST?

The International Society for Technology in Education (ISTE®) is an association for educators and education leaders for the effective use of technology in PK-12 and teacher education.

About NETS Standards & Benchmarks

ISTE's National Educational Technology Standards (NETS) a roadmap since 1998 for improved learning and teaching. NETS helps measure proficiency and set goals for students (NETS•S), teachers (NETS•T), and administrators (NETS•A) dealing with technology in education. Their leadership in developing benchmarks and guiding implementation has resulted in broad adoption of ISTE's standards in the U.S. and many other countries.

Reference: National Educational Technology Standards for Students, Second Edition, ©2007, ISTE® (International Society for Technology in Education), www.iste.org. All rights reserved.

Technology Without a Technology Coordinator

The ideal situation is to not have a technology coordinator on staff. Teachers should be using technology in the classroom in a transparent manner. There should not be time set aside for the instruction of devices nor programs. All instruction pertaining to technology should be integrated into core subject lessons. The

Technology Extension Map is designed as a guide for teachers to use to enhance their core curriculum lessons.

The STEM (science, technology, engineering and math) based curriculum map is designed for independent units to be taught in the classroom with technology as the main focus. These skills are vital for understanding the basic foundations of our world and how technology is intertwined into all aspects of a modern society.

Technology should be device and software independent. In other words, any reference to technology in the classroom should be based on skills not brand names, and any task should be open to any device or software. The goal is to be device independent. Internet based software should be emphasized.

Technology Extension Map

Similar to a curriculum map, the extension map is designed for use in conjunction with a core unit curriculum map to enhance it in regards to the use of technology. It should be very general and open to interpretation as to which device and software to use. More importantly the scope of skills should easily be accomplished within an academic school year, and should be very basic. It should not be based on early adoption devices or software, only on topics that are relevant for the foreseeable future.

Grade Level	K-2	3-5	6-8	9-12
Basic Operations	Introduction User Interfaces, Basic usage of system software	Proficiency, online navigation of online tools	Proficiency online tools primary use	Mastery Complete online use, location free
Research	Introduction to simple aspects of paraphrasing and citation	Proficiency, basic citation requirements	Proficiency, introduction to more advanced forms of citation	Mastery, full citation
Common Sense, CyberSMART	Introduction to self awareness of personal identity	Introduction of social media, Cyberbullying	Proficiency of social media	Mastery Advocacy of online awareness
System Based Productivity Suites	Introduction	Proficiency	Mastery	NA Due to Students should be System Free
Online Tools	NA Due to Parent Involvement	Introduction	Proficiency	Mastery

STEM Units Based Curriculum Map

There are topics dealing with technology that should be taught as a stand alone units. These are topics that are vital for the future of all modern economies and corresponding workforces. The units should be evenly spaced out throughout the K-12 map, to ensure a building of knowledge and skill sets. As students move through a school vertically, the STEM based skills should be incrementally added, and considered mastered and utilized as they are completed.

Grade Level	K-2	3-5	6-8	9-12
Science	Basic circuitry made for young children	Basic concepts of energy, simple circuitry projects	Exploration of energy manipulation, circuitry projects	Advanced concepts energy manipulation, advanced circuitry projects
Technology	System based tools	Online Tools	Location free devices	Projects incorporating all devices across multiple applications
Engineering	Simple Toys such as Kinects	Introduction Arduino / Lego Mindstorm	Arduino / Lego Mindstorm	Arduino / Lego Mindstorm
Math	Online simple programming	Visual Programming Languages	Introduction to web based programming	Java, .NET, Andriod, iOS

STEM Integration

Often schools prefer to use an integration model as opposed to a unit based timeline. The benefits of a more loose knit structure is the freedom of choice for teachers allowing them to take advantage of locally accessible supplies, current themes, and curriculum. In addition teachers are always more self motivated when given the freedom of choice, making more likely the integration of STEM concepts. It is best to not think of STEM literally when planning, but instead think of three key components that are in all intents and purposes STEM, CREATION, LOGIC, and RESEARCH. All projects or units can easily uses these three keys and fulfill the STEM requirements.

- STEM is only an initiative
- Try to incorporate STEM into projects
- Logic Research Creation
  - Creation using concepts of study
  - Logic, order procedural operations
  - Research, finding/locating information

Lesson Format

Having a standard lesson format to follow, helps students as well as it keeps a class routine organized. There are many parts to a lesson, but every teacher does it differently. The most important aspect of a lesson format is consistency. Below are some common components of a lesson.

1. Goal
2. Standards and Benchmarks
3. Stated Objective - Let students know what they will be doing.
4. Body - include teacher notes to self as well as step by step instructions, should include a vocabulary and differentiation sections.
5. Reflection - this part if often left out, but is a great addition especially if you plan to revisit at a later time.

Having a lesson plan documented also helps in case you need a substitute.

Lesson Format Revealer

Utilizing technology where the curriculum play a major part and the technology aspect plays a supporting role is a fundamental structure of any project. The revealer project involves a higher level of thinking and can utilize technology skills at every level.

- Have subject
- Create two sections of project (any format, such as video, presentation, or document)
  - Description of informative
  - Answer or revealing aspect
- presentation (can be online, or offline)
- Audience participation in guessing/reflecting on subject matter topic (email, reflection, commenting)

Lessons

When planning out units for a year, consider using ISTE's NETS standards for the unit topics. All six standards should be covered within a school year and may overlap or be repeated. The six standards are as follow,

1. Basic Operations
2. Digital Citizenship
3. Research
4. Critical Thinking
5. Creativity
6. Communication

The Core units which are mapped out in the Pacing Guide, or lessons that should be taught in all grade levels as they are the basic skills and content needed to ensure that students are prepared.

Making a cheat sheets or posting student friendly summaries is important so students can refer back to the main ideas or points of each lesson taught.

Suggested/Mandatory Core Lessons

The suggested core units include lessons that are important and should be taught within the elementary years. Some teachers may argue that they are not needed as the topics are not really important or useful for what they plan to achieve. This is not a valid argument, as students may need the covered skills in other classrooms. In addition, many of the skills spill over into the private lives of students. Having the skills and background knowledge early on in their lives can only help, not hinder their development. Also, once teachers see what can be achieved with technology, they may come up with or want to incorporate the skills into their curriculum or projects.

Secondary students should also have mandatory lessons or blocked classes in transitional years to help move them in a socially responsible direction in regards to technology use. Middle school years should be focusing on the use of technology targeted towards individual and inner circle appropriate use. High school students should start to expand their focus to the impact of technology into the greater society.

Basic Skills

Basic skill should be taught before many of the other units to insure that time is not wasted stepping backwards in the sequence plan. It is important to try and teach as many of the basic skills as possible as many teachers will want to start collaborative projects early in the year, especially for holiday projects.

Here are topics that should be covered. They are in no particular order, and they should be platform independent.

1. The first aspect of basic skills that needs to be explaining how to move to workstations or how to line up to get out the devices without crowding.
2. Demonstrate what to do to get attention of the class. There are many ways to do this, but they almost all involve making it so students can't see their screens. This helps maintain their attention.
3. Next demonstrated is logging in and out.
4. Input control and working on hand-eye coordination.
5. Where to find programs, using a menu, folder, or search function.
6. Starting and stopping programs.
7. Basic vocabulary.

Commenting

Teaching students how to communicate using social media is a skill that needs to be taught, just as speech is taught as a crucial skill. Below are some of the problems encountered in regards to communicating online, and would make for some perfect lessons on communicating online.

Personal Attacks
It's ok to disagree, but don't make it personal.

Professing Your Love and Lust
Stay professional and remember others will see your post. Nothing is private online.

Off-Topic Discussion
Keep on topic, remember to stay focused on one idea.

Annoying the Hell Out of Everyone
tacky expressions gets tiresome to many. Avoid over used phrases and Internet abbreviations.

Trolling
Being mean to others for no purpose is called trolling. Don't do it.

Whining About Content
If you don't like the subject matter being written about, skip it and come back later. Don't waste people times by complaining about it.

Obnoxious Corrections
People make mistakes. it's not OK to be point out mistakes in a non-constructive manner and insult others.

The AUTOBAN List
below is a list of things that will usually get you banned from a web site,

- Commenting just to say "First!"
- Comments with little more than LOL, LMAO, THIS, tl;dr, or equivalent
- **Repeated or multiple** comments with nothing but an image
- "Slow news day?" or equivalent
- Graphic or disgusting images
- Spam or malicious links
- Revealing personal information (such as addresses, phone numbers, etc) of others

Reference: Gizmodo

Device Input

Track Pads

Using a laptop trackpad is a skill that needs to be practiced just like a keyboard or mouse. For younger students it can be very difficult. Even adults often have difficulty with the fine coordination skills needed. A good tip to help students use a trackpad id to have them use one hand only. This forces them to pick up their finger before clicking, which often cause problems. Students have a tendency to move their finger on the trackpad as they click. Also, they have trouble coordinating two fingers as they track across the pad.

Touch Devices

Many devices are moving to touch screens as a means of control. Even though touch is not always the best means of controlling a device, it is very intuitive especially for younger students. However the limitation of touch become evident with inputing large quantities of text. Finger fatigue can be an issue when students are unable to rest their fingers as when using a keyboard. An alternative to using a pencil or pen is stylus enabled devices which allow students to write notes or input large quantities of text as if the device were a journal or piece of paper.

Mouse or Track Ball

Mice and trackpad devices have been around for many years and are considered by many as the ideal method of control for any computing device. An important aspect that should be taken into consideration when choosing devices is the size of the the students using the device. Laptop mice are ideal if the students are young. Also, even when using Macs, PC mice are a great alternative to Mac mice as the buttons are intuitive and easier to direct students to their use. A hybrid touch mice are also making their way into the market and combine the touch and movement of mice for an interesting combination. Just be aware the size is an issue when choosing equipment for younger students.

Kinesthetic Movement

Controlling devices with body gestures is starting to make their way onto the market. These devices and controllers will add an interesting mix to teaching in the classroom. When adopting a new technology be sure to pilot it to work out any unforeseen issues or problems.

Due Diligence

The goal of most bad elements on the Internet is to gain access to your email, personal information, and your money. These bad elements have used many techniques over the years to gain access to private information, but now due to the ever present threat, most companies have put a stop to the old fashioned direct approach. Instead they use social engineering to gain access. People making mistakes or being tricked is how they gain access.

The easiest way to prevent being tricked is to practice due diligence, staying on well known popular sites and staying away from more shady sites will eliminate most of your threats.

Practicing safe searching and having a strong password on your accounts is another way to prevent being taken advantage of even though brute force attacks on passwords is no longer common. Downloading malware is by far the most dangerous threat today. If malware is loaded onto your computer, it will load what is called a keylogger which will steal your private account information from your computer.

One easy trick is to never have your computer "remember" or "save" your password. Connivence usually comes back to bite you in the long run.

- Social Engineering
- Shady Web Sites
- Passwords
- Keyloggers

Email

Email is a fast and convenient way to communicate and is a big part of our everyday life. We use it increasingly more in school to communicate with peers and teachers, and to share information in a more formal way other than chatting or using social media.

Teaching how to use email should follow a thoughtful process to ensure that students are prepared for its proper use.

Stage One

Students should all be required to complete an email expectations discussion. The discussion should center around appropriate use, safety, and responsibility.

Stage Two

Just like other forms of writing, there is a format to follow and the writing process can be applied. Students should be required to follow a Friendly Letter Format. This is more a safety issue than a language arts issue. Malicious software to this day is unable to create personalized emails using a Friendly Letter Format. This is the only true preventative measure available to protect the receiver of emails.

Before you write:
- Know your goal (What is the reason you are writing?)
- Think about the recipient of your message (Teacher or friend)

During writing:
- Fill in the Subject Line - Make sure it is informative
- Greet the reader – politely say hello and tell why you are writing
- Organize your details
- Close Politely

After writing:
- Read your message carefully
- Make sure your writing is complete and correct before hitting send.

ISTE's NETS Standards and Benchmarks
Communication and Collaboration
- communicate information and ideas effectively to multiple audiences using a variety of media and formats.

Digital Citizenship
- advocate and practice safe, legal, and responsible use of information and technology.

- exhibit a positive attitude toward using technology that supports collaboration, learning, and productivity.

Good Presentations

Creating a good presentation regardless of what application used can be a difficult thing to do. Typically, we go overboard when making presentations, keeping it simple is the best advice in creating a presentation that doesn't lose or bore your audience. Below are some tips for creating or teaching students how to make a worthy presentation.
- No more than one idea per slide. If you have more than one idea per slide, consider using a different format such as a report, rather than a presentation.
- Avoid clipart and common sayings. Take your time to come up with solid relationships of ideas.
- Your slide shouldn't take more than 3 seconds to comprehend.
- Use simple smart designs. Don't use random images, and make sure your colors and contrast are clean.
- Make sure that the presentation is meaningful "W.I.I.F.M. - what's in it for me?"

Remember: Less is more!

Good Web Sites

A good web page to use for a resource:
1. You can read most of the words: it should not have more than 5 words you can't read.
2. No ads: some ads are ok, but if there are more then two, find another site.
3. You can find the Author: if it is a gov or org site it is ok. Also the copyright at the bottom is ok for the author as well.
4. Date it was made: The copyright date will do for the date.
5. The right type of information (fact or opinion)

Look at each of the following pages and find the page (s) that are best for writing a factual report on a country.
1. http://en.wikipedia.org/wiki/Portugal
2. http://www.infoplease.com/ipa/A0107895.html
3. http://www.portugal.com/portugal/
4. http://kids.yahoo.com/reference/world-factbook/country/po--Portugal
5. http://www.soschildrensvillages.ca/Where-we-help/Europe/Portugal/Pages/default.aspx

Reflection: Which page was the best for you to use, why?

Google Earth

Demonstrate to students the use of Google Earth. It is best to have a hands on activity ready so students can follow along.

Basic Topics to be covered in the introduction lessons.

Lesson 1
- Navigation Controls, Look, Pan and Elevation. R=reset.
- SEARCH Panel, Fly To should be selected, then enter address, Proper Place Name, or coordinates. Can double-click any previous found place or drag-drop it into Places Folder for saving. Clear button is useful to reset search results so it's not cluttered.

- LAYERS Panel, Have students turn on Photos and More>Wikipedia. This turns GE into a places based search engine. Make sure you go over what they should do if they inadvertently come across inappropriate content.

Lesson 2
- PLACES Panel, You can turn off and on places and drag and drop them into the My Places folder for long term storage. Create Folders.
- Placemark, Properties or Get Info allows for editing pins.
- Save Place As, creates a file that can be shared via email with others, or embed the KML link.

Lesson 3 & 4
- Tours, allow for direct display of content. Make sure that "*Show balloon while waiting*" is checked in the preferences. TIP: Each place mark needs to have an image inserted in order for the balloon to show when waiting at a place-mark.

Intermediate Topics / Lesson Ideas
- Language Arts
  - Street View /Peg Man, 3D Building should be activated in the the LAYERS Panel. Have students write about living in a particular city writing about what they see and can do.
- Science
  - 3D Trees, available for most parks around the world. Have students compare vegetation of different climates.
  - Sun, Moon, Planets and Stars, can all be explored as well.
- Social Studies
  - Historical View, see what places looked like back in time. Have students explore how cities change with time.
- Social Studies / Language Arts
  - Have students create a Path that follows a historical figure. They can create multiple paths and style them differently to distinguish between them. They can write about the significance of the path in the description.
  - Polygons can also be made to show areas of influence, or where certain events took place. Once saved, they can be exported and sent to teacher for review.
- Math
  - The Polygon and Measure tools can be used to measure area and distance between places. Comparing and contrasting is a way to combine language arts benchmarks as well.
- All Subjects
  - Create a tour of placemarks, paths, and or polygons. The timing settings can be adjusted to go slower if needed.
  - Pre-made tours can be used for many subject areas, just click on the Earth Gallery button in the Layers Panel.
- PE
  - Track distance of hike or run.

Internet Safety

Bad Web Site Tricks

Do not click on any Game Ads on web sites. Especially if they promise you money or free stuff. These web sites will sometimes load a Virus onto your computer and turn it into a zombie!

Spam Tricks

Beware of emails ask you to FORWARD an email to your friends for good luck. The spammers are trying to get your friends email addresses! If you forward the email, it will send the spammer the email as well and they will steal all the email addresses of your friends.

Keyboarding

Keyboarding is an important skill *Wetzel (1985)* that is taught using one of two programs. For Kinder through 2nd grade, use the program Tux Typing if you school uses PC's, as Tux Typing is easy for younger students to use. Also, it allows for custom word lists, to help with homeroom collaboration. If your school uses Macs, and you have good Internet connectivity, use the web based Dance Mat Typing from the BBC web site. The goal for K-2 is familiarization and basic techniques *Nieman (1996)*. For 3rd through 5th we use a more comprehensive typing program such as All the Right Type, which is a client server based program for the PC. Non-web based typing programs often allow for tracking of student progress, unlike most of the online typing programs. For the Mac Mavis Beacon has a program that can be loaded on your school network. The goal is to have students learn basic typing skills using programs, then to incorporate the skills learned into existing projects where they can practice what they have learned.

After students achieve grade level WPM level, they will continue keyboarding familiarization using leveled word lists.

Three Areas of Importance for Typing
1. Posture - Students need to learn good posture while typing to decrease fatigue *Nieman (1996)*
2. Home Row - Insuring that students keep their fingers on the home row will help them become efficient *Nieman (1996)*
3. No looking - Taking the time to look for keys demonstrates that more practice is needed. *Nieman (1996)*

WPM - 3rd grade aims for **15wpm**, 4th grade aims for **20wpm**, and 5th grade will aim for **30wpm** *Sormunen (1988, 1991, 1993)*

Keyboarding Teaching Tip

When students are typing, they will tend to pick-up their hand in order to reach key certain keys such as Backspace. Allowing them to do so will hobble their ability to achieve a high typing rate. Show students that they can reach far-away keys, but have them keep their pointing finger on the initial home row keys J and F. This will allow them to quickly place their other fingers back on the home row keys.
To help students learn to type without looking at the keyboard, have them use the on-screen virtual keyboard common with most typing programs. If the program you are using doesn't have an on-screen prompt, you should think about getting or using a different program.
Also, once students are taught Home Row, use a piece of felt or folded paper to cover their hands. This in conjunction with the online screen visual can really help them quickly learn proper finger placement.

Links to Online Typing Tests & Lessons

Online Keyboarding Test Grades 2-12
Online Keyboarding Lessons Grades 2-5
Dance Mat Typing Lessons Grades K-2

Nieman, P. (1996). Introducing early keyboard skills: Who, what, where, and how?. Business Education Forum, 51(1), 27-30.
Sormunen, C. (1988). A comparison of speed achievement of students in grades 3-6 who learn keyboarding on the microcomputer. The Delta Pi Epsilon Journal, 30(2), 47-57.
Sormunen, C. (1991). Elementary school keyboarding: A case for skill development. Business Education Forum, 45(6), 28-30. Retrieved January 30, 2005 from Utah State University, Business Information Systems and Education Department website:
http://www.usoe.k12.ut.us/ate/keyboarding/Articles/EKcase.htm

Sormunen, C. (1993). Learning style: An analysis of factors affecting keyboarding achievement of elementary school students. The Delta Pi Epsilon Journal, 35(1), 26-38.

Classroom Differentiation

As for differentiating instruction, the keyboarding lessons can differentiate in regards to *students* and between classes. Using the keyboarding lessons as a filler class enables teachers to keep the scope and sequence in order. This gives classes that are behind schedule for whatever reason time to catch up.

Online Tools

The use of online tools, otherwise known as Web 2.0, is a easy way to incorporate the latest technology skills into ones curriculum. Google Apps, Zoho, or Microsoft Groove are just a few of the tools available, which allow for an online collaborative environment.

Google Apps in the Classroom

Google apps is one of the easiest tools for incorporation of technology in the classroom. The benefits include the ability to work from anywhere, with anyone, at anytime, and to do it at the same time. Below are listed the highlights of introducing the use of Google Apps in the classroom.

- Have students create together with the teacher a gmail account. Explain to students that you will have access to their account and that it is not private and for school use only. Tell them that you will periodically check the account for inappropriate use. However, one should only randomly and very infrequently check the account as policing them is a waste of time and resources.
- Have students send an email to the teacher so a connection between the gmail accounts can be established. This will make sharing of documents easier later on.
- Demonstrate how to create and share a document. Explain the revision history aspect in part so students know that what they do can be seen by everyone. This will head off any inappropriate use later on.
- Have students work collaboratively in a classroom environment so they become familiar with it's use.

First Steps & Tips

- Stat Google apps with introduction to Gmail. Gmail is part of the suite of applications that will be available to students. Prior explanation of email basics and behavior expectations is a must. The earlier the grade level the more detail and time will be need for this stage of introduction.
- Explain browser tabs. Using tabs makes managing the different windows much easier.
- Have students change password and notify teacher via email of their new passwords.
- Demonstrate the use of Google Docs. Explanation of the document list view is critical. Also, explain the different types of documents that can be created and shared.
- Explain the chat feature and its use. Re-explanation of behavior expectations will be needed especially with younger students.
- Demonstrate and explain the Commenting Feature.
- Explain the different options for sharing and that each project must have a project leader. The project leader is the student who creates the document.

Print & Digital Resources

Goal: Students will demonstrate their ability to understand the benefits and drawbacks of using print and online research tools, by comparing and contrasting the two.

Body: Have students use both Digital and Print resources for a search subject.

Demonstrate the use of Google's Advanced search where the reading level can be specified.

Productivity Software

One of the most basic aspects of teaching technology is to prepare students in such a way that they can utilize any system to create a product. The product can be anything related to learning and there are more specialized software programs for specific products that teachers may want to create. However the basics for any classroom should be the a word processor, presentation software, and a number manipulation software. Any productivity suite should work fine. A matter of fact, students should be taught the productivity software in such a way that they can take the skills learned and use any of the software packages available regardless of platform.

For older students, steering them to the use of online collaborative productivity software is far more ideal than using a stand alone suite such as iWork, Microsoft Office, or Open Source suites such as Openoffice. Online suite offers almost all of the bells and whistles of stand alone suites with the added benefit of online access and collaborative functionality.

The best option if a school has good Internet connectivity is to use Google Docs for all word processing. The collaboration and accessibility option are untouched by all the other software suites available.

Things to know for 3rd thru 5th Grade
1. Where to find word processor program
2. Create new document
3. Name at top of document
4. Title should be underlined and have Heading Style
5. Font = Times New Roman
6. Size = 14
7. Use Save As to save to specific location and to give revision name

Research Project

(Big 6 step 1 Task Definition: determine the information needed)
Create a wiki page for the Research Project.
Pick a Topic: The subject area is **Famous Explorers**. You may pick an explorer of your choice. Record your Explorer's name on your wiki

Put your heading here in bold print (Your explorer's name, for example: **JOHN STANLEY)**

1.) 3 Keywords *(Big6 Step 2: determine all possible sources)* i).   ii).   iii).
NOTE: *Leveling:* **Is the resource you found too hard to understand? If yes, find another source. Use the 5 Word Rule to find out.**
NOTE: *Citing Sources*: **Remember, during research, list all your sources.**
NOTE: **Verify your Source: Ask yourself, "Can you find your fact in one other place?"**
Using Keywords:
   1A: Online Library Catalog search for print sources using keywords: *I found/did not find a lot of information. It was hard/easy to find specific information.*
   1B: Encyclopedia search using keywords: *I found/did not find a lot of information. It was hard/easy to find specific information.*
   1C: Online Google search using keywords: *I found/did not find a lot of information. It was hard/easy to find specific information.*

2.) 3 Key Phrases *(Big6 Step 2: determine all possible sources)* i).   ii).   iii).
NOTE: *Leveling:* **Is the resource you found too hard to understand? If yes, find another source. Use the 5 Word Rule to find out.**
NOTE: *Citing Sources*: **Remember, during research, list all your sources.**

NOTE: Verify your Source: Ask yourself, "Can you find your fact in one other place?"
Using Keyphrases:
    2A: Catalog search for print sources, using key phrases: I found/did not find a lot of information. It was hard/easy to find specific information.
        2B: Do an encyclopedia search using your key phrases: I found/did not find a lot of information. It was hard/easy to find specific information.
    2C: Do an online Google search using your key phrases: I found/did not find a lot of information. It was hard/easy to find specific information.

3.) Reflection Keyword Vs. Keyphrase (Big 6 Step 6: Evaluate the process and the product)
 How did the results of your research change by using keywords versus using key phrases?

4.) Reflection Print Vs. Online (Big6 Step 6: Evaluate the process and the product)
1. A *drawback* for using **online** resources for research is (complete the sentence)
2. A *benefit* for using **online** resources for research is (complete the sentence)
3. A *drawback* for using **print** resources for research is (complete the sentence)
4. A *benefit* for using **print** resources for research is (complete the sentence)
5. The sources that worked better **for my topic**, were ... (complete the sentence Give reasons why you think so. Some examples of reasons might be: source includes graphics; source has more specific information; source has relevant information; source uses simpler language; information is clearly organized; source is easy to navigate; all information is located in one place; etc. Think of other reasons why one source of information would work better for you than another).

5.) Product Put your sub-topic here in bold print. (Big 6 Step 6: Evaluate the process and the product) (for example: **Exploring the Nile with John Stanley)** write a paragraph **on your wiki** explaining the importance of your explorer. Include a graphic. (Big6 Steps 3-5: Locate, use and synthesize information)
(i). Web site: (copy and paste at least one URL that you used here)
(ii). Print source: (write your book's title, author and year of publication here)

Resources
Sources of information:
Print: Discovery Encyclopedia; World Book; Library catalog to search for non-fiction books.
Online: gogrolier / learn Grolier Online; Ask; Wikipedia;
http://americanhistory.mrdonn.org/explorers.html;http://www.elizabethan-era.org.uk/famous-explorers.htm;

Research Web Skills

Project Info Lit's Alison J. Head, recently stated that the results from their work show that today's students struggle with a feeling of information overload.

Aspects of Web Research
Students should first try to use a kid friendly search site before using more adult oriented sites such as Google. If Google is used, make sure that the safe search filtering is set to **strict**. This is not perfect, but will prevent some of the adult content from being viewed.

Before they start, they must know what they are looking for! Have students prepare by brainstorming keywords and phrases.

Have students use a kid safe Search Engine such as Ask for Kids. There are a number of child friendly search engines and directories to use. However, many of them do not filter results based on reading level. Google's Advanced Search will allow one to filter based on reading level, but the user interface is designed for adults and less intuitive.

Almost all web search sites using Google's search engine. This can be a positive aspect as it adds uniformity in the output generated by the search engine. If it is indeed Google Search engine, the results page should contain a title and blurb. Teaching students how to read the title and blurbs will help them quickly determine if the result is what they are looking for. If they get to the end of the search result page and they haven't found any relevant sites, have them revise their search phrase and try again.

Scanning

Scanning is an important skill as well. Have students look for bold or italic words within the search results and within the website itself. This skill can be difficult to learn in the early years but should be taught and practiced often. Another quick and easy way to help students with scanning a web page is to use the Find Function. On the Apple, Linux, and Microsoft operating systems, it is found in the Edit pull-down menu.

Booleans

Using booleans such as AND, NOT, and OR can help refine a search and save a great deal of time.
- AND can be used to include additional keywords to a search string. Usually the actual word "and" doesn't have to be written but is assumed if more than one word is used. The plus sign can also be used but is also redundant.
- NOT is used to filter results. If a search result produces unwanted content, just add the "not" boolean then add the key word or phrase of the unwanted result. The word "not" or the minus sign can be used.
- OR can be used to widen a search result.

Distinguishing the Difference Between Search Engines & Search Directories

One word search: Have students do a one word search using a noun. Have them take note of the top three web sites that come up and how many pages were found.
Short Phrase Search: Have students now use a short phrase nouns with adjectives, and do the same as above.

Using Quotes: Now have them use quotes and compare results with not using them.
Results: Can you understand what you found? If, not don't use it! 5 Word Rule.

Using Google advance search will allow for the use of the reading level option. This will help ensure that students find appropriately leveled material. Have students try filtering the results using Google's Readability filter.

Now use a Directory such as kids.yahoo.com, and compare the amount of results.

Is the Information Good?

Finding information that is valid can be a problem especially for students. using the following three questions should help them determine if the information they have found is good. In addition, have students look for the same fact or information on another web site in which the information is worded differently.
1. Who wrote it? Clue, look for the domain suffix. Is it ".edu" or ".gov"?
2. What type of information is it, Opinions or Facts? Opinions are useful, but you need to know the difference.
3. When was the web page created? Make sure that there is not better, newer information available.

Plagiarism

To avoid and to train students about plagiarism , have them always cite the web page they used to get their information. Each grade level should have different requirements for citation. Even children as young as kindergarten should start the citation process, for example by noting the letter of what they were searching for on the back of the worksheet they are using or digitally in the document they create.
Paraphrasing is also an important skill that should be learned and reinforced. If students copy and paste, they

need to learn to use proper citation such as using quotes and listing where they found the information by citing the URL or web address of the information found.

Research Web Skills Tips for Students

Project Info Lit's Alison J. Head, recently stated that the results from their work show that today's students struggle with a feeling of information overload.

Aspects of Web Research

Students should first try to use a kid friendly search site before using more adult oriented sites such as Google. If Google is used, make sure that the safe search filtering is set to **strict**. This is not perfect, but will prevent some of the adult content from being viewed.

Before they start, they must know what they are looking for! Have students prepare by brainstorming keywords and phrases.

Have students use a kid safe Search Engine such as Ask for Kids. There are a number of child friendly search engines and directories to use. However, many of them do not filter results based on reading level. Google's Advanced Search will allow one to filter based on reading level, but the user interface is designed for adults and less intuitive.

Almost all web search sites using Google's search engine. This can be a positive aspect as it adds uniformity in the output generated by the search engine. If it is indeed Google Search engine, the results page should contain a title and blurb. Teaching students how to read the title and blurbs will help them quickly determine if the result is what they are looking for. If they get to the end of the search result page and they haven't found any relevant sites, have them revise their search phrase and try again.

Scanning

Scanning is an important skill as well. Have students look for bold or italic words within the search results and within the website itself. This skill can be difficult to learn in the early years but should be taught and practiced often. Another quick and easy way to help students with scanning a web page is to use the Find Function. On the Apple, Linux, and Microsoft operating systems, it is found in the Edit pull-down menu.

Booleans

Using booleans such as AND, NOT, and OR can help refine a search and save a great deal of time.
- AND can be used to include additional keywords to a search string. Usually the actual word "and" doesn't have to be written but is assumed if more than one word is used. The plus sign can also be used but is also redundant.
- NOT is used to filter results. If a search result produces unwanted content, just add the "not" boolean then add the key word or phrase of the unwanted result. The word "not" or the minus sign can be used.
- OR can be used to widen a search result.

Distinguishing the Difference Between Search Engines & Search Directories

One word search: Have students do a one word search using a noun. Have them take note of the top three web sites that come up and how many pages were found.
Short Phrase Search: Have students now use a short phrase nouns with adjectives, and do the same as above.

Using Quotes: Now have them use quotes and compare results with not using them.
Results: Can you understand what you found? If, not don't use it! 5 Word Rule.

Using Google advance search will allow for the use of the reading level option. This will help ensure that students find appropriately leveled material. Have students try filtering the results using Google's Readability filter.

Now use a Directory such as kids.yahoo.com, and compare the amount of results.

Is the Information Good?
Finding information that is valid can be a problem especially for students. using the following three questions should help them determine if the information they have found is good. In addition, have students look for the same fact or information on another web site in which the information is worded differently.
1. Who wrote it? Clue, look for the domain suffix. Is it ".edu" or ".gov"?
2. What type of information is it, Opinions or Facts? Opinions are useful, but you need to know the difference.
3. When was the web page created? Make sure that there is not better, newer information available.

Plagiarism

To avoid and to train students about plagiarism , have them always cite the web page they used to get their information. Each grade level should have different requirements for citation. Even children as young as kindergarten should start the citation process, for example by noting the letter of what they were searching for on the back of the worksheet they are using or digitally in the document they create.

Paraphrasing is also an important skill that should be learned and reinforced. If students copy and paste, they need to learn to use proper citation such as using quotes and listing where they found the information by citing the URL or web address of the information found.

Scanning
Fact Gathering Step
1. Read paragraph all the way through.
2. Read each individual sentence one at a time.
3. Look at each sentence and pick out important words that you understand.
4. Write each important word down as a complete sentence.
5. Re-read each sentence you wrote and line-out any words you cannot explain to your teacher.

How to find what you are looking for,
1. Just like book: just by how it looks, does the web page look like it will have the information you are looking for?
2. Keywords: look for the keyword of what you are looking for without reading!
3. Search function: use CTRL + F to enact the search function, then use a keyword or phrase to pinpoint where the keyword is on the page.
4. Pictures: Look for pictures to guide you to what you are looking for.
5. Navigation Links: look for a link in the navigation bar at the top or left-hand side of the web page to guide you.

Tips
- Look at result page for bold words that you used
- Read the brief description before clicking on link
- rephrase your search words
- Use a question as your search phrase, maybe some else had the same question

Search Exercise

Use a search engine such as Ask Jeeves or Google.
1. Pick a noun on a topic you are studying, and enter it in the search box. Look at the top 3 web pages that come up. How many pages were found?
2. Use the root of the noun and see if it changes the results.
3. Use the same noun, but add a modifier (adjective) and do the search again. Notice if any of the top three pages change. How many pages were found, and are the results better?
4. Now add another noun or modifier, and do the search again. How many pages were found, and are the results better?
5. Now try adding quotes to part or all of your search phrase. How many pages were found, and are the results even better?
6. Try changing the order of the words and phrases used. How many pages were found, and are the results better?
7. How about capital letters? Do they change the result?

Reflection: What have you learned?

Trustworthy Site

Is this a Legitimate or Trustworthy Web Site?
Sometimes we come across a website with what appears to be good information. The question we should ask is whether or not the information is valid. Follow the link to the following web site and complete the Webquest

http://teachertech.rice.edu/participants/bchristo/lessons/evalwebsites

VoiceThread

Learning to speak is a skill that sometimes is not emphasized enough in international schools. In schools where the language of instruction is not that of the host country, students spend as little as 3% of the school year speaking the language of instruction. This is far too little in order to help students become fluent speakers.

With the use of a multitude of free voice recording software, students can easily dictate work that they already have written in order to practice their speaking skills. In addition reading ones work aloud is one of the best ways to proofread work during the edit and revise stage of the writing process.

Once students have a finished piece of writing, have them dictate their work and record it for later publication in a digital portfolio. Parents and students alike enjoy and take pride in listening to the improvement in speaking skills over a period of time, which the oral presentations can deliver.

DAY 1
What is VoiceThread?
- Voicethread is a web based program, you need the Internet to use it.
- Your voicethread account is like an email account.

Responsible Use
- Nothing is Private
- No take-backs! Be polite.

Menus: Browse, Create, and My Voice
- Each voicethread is a square thumbnail image.
- Voice Moderation (yellow for unheard, gray is hidden.)

Create a voicethread.
- Find and insert an image
- write a sentence
- Save and Explain naming conventions

DAY 2
Review Responsible Use
Share a voicethread.
Have students watch a voicethread and leave a comment.
Doodle.

	Accomplished	Proficient	Intermediate	Beginner
Word Choice	Speaker's choice of language and uses of voice is descriptive, interesting, and well worded.	Speaker's choice of language and use of voice is interesting and well worded.	Speaker's choice of language and use of voice is interesting.	Speaker participates in VoiceThread activity.
Innovation or Interest level	Speaker creatively presents meaningful sequences of events.	Speaker creatively presents meaningful events.	Speaker presents meaningful events.	Speaker presents events.
Timing and Pace	The speaker's story is presented accurately, with natural rests and keeps the listeners' interest throughout.	The speaker's story is presented accurately, and keeps the listeners' interest throughout.	The speaker's story is presented accurately, and keeps the listeners' interest for the most part.	The speaker's story is presented accurately.
Focus	Speaker's comments add to the focus, and interest. Comments are well constructed, thoughtful and productive	Speaker's comments add to the focus, interest, and the comments are constructive and thoughtful	Speaker's comments add to the focus, interest, and are thoughtful	Speaker's comments are thoughtful

Leveled Lesson Ideas

Kindergarten Lessons
- Computer lab expectations
- Keyboarding (key familiarity)
- Learn to Use a Mouse: Use online website to teach mouse skills.
- Learn to Use a Paint Program: Use paint program to learn about toolbar, and practice mouse skills.
- Learn to Use a Program. Have students learn to log in and start a paint program.
- Mind Mapping Create: Use software to practice mouse skills by selecting and organizing.
- Web Site Use: Use an educational web site.

1st Grade
- Computer lab expectations
- Paint Program: Basic computer usage including logging on and off, starting and stopping program.
- Keyboarding: (home row familiarity)
- Mind Mapping: Sorting and labeling
- PM Reader: Use of PM Reader program.
- Simple Presentation: Use of presentation program to record voice
- Web Site Use: Use an educational web site.

2nd Grade
- Computer lab expectations
- Internet Smarts
- Keyboarding: (home row and focus on screen)
- Paint Program: Basic computer usage including logging on and off, starting and stopping program.
- Mind Mapping: Sorting and labeling
- Mind Mapping: Writing Process
- Simple Presentation: Use of presentation program to record voice
- Web Site Use: Use an educational web site.
- Word Processing: Use word processor to create document.
- Digital Portfolios: Use presentation software to create trimester based digital portfolio.
- Email: Introduction of email use.
- Researching Skills
- Friendly Letter Format

3rd Grade
- Computer lab expectations
- Internet Smarts
- Web Site Use: Use an educational web site.
- Keyboarding (10-15 WPM)
- Email: Introduction of email use and expectations.
- Digital Portfolios: Use presentation software to create trimester based digital portfolio.
- Word Processing: Use word processor to create document.
- Presentation Software
- Movie Production
- Researching Skills
- Mind Mapping: Writing Process
- Social Media Exploration (social media expectations)

4th Grade
- Computer lab expectations

- Internet Smarts
- Web Site Use: Use an educational web site.
- Keyboarding: (20-25 WPM)
- Email: (review email basic and exceptions)
- Digital Image Manipulation Beginning
- Digital Portfolios: Use presentation software to create trimester based digital portfolio.
- Word Processing: Use word processor to create document.
- Presentation Software
- Movie Production
- Researching Skills
- Mind Mapping: Writing Process
- Social Media (social media expectations)

5th Grade
- Computer lab expectations
- Internet Smarts
- Web Site Use: Use an educational web site.
- Keyboarding: (30 WPM)
- Email (Web 2.0)
- Digital Image Manipulation
- Digital Portfolios: Use presentation software to create trimester based digital portfolio.
- Word Processing: Use word processor to create document.
- Presentation Software
- Spreadsheet Program
- Movie Production
- Audacity
- Researching Skills
- Mind Mapping: Writing Process
- Social Media (social media expectations)
- Google Earth

Pacing Guide

Pacing Guide 1st Grade			
	Topics	Skills/Knowledge	Assessment Strategy
August	Basic Operations and Concepts, Log On/Off, Lab rules	Basic input devices Classroom rules	Observational Scoring Rubrics
September	Keyboarding	Common menu items	Observational Scoring Rubrics
October	Productivity Tools,	Basic drawing tool box	Observational

	Graphics	items	Scoring Rubrics
November	Social, Ethical, and Human Issues	Social responsibilities	Observational Scoring Rubrics
December	Social, Ethical, and Human Issues	Social responsibilities	Observational Scoring Rubrics
January	Social, Ethical, and Human Issues	Social responsibilities	Observational Scoring Rubrics
February	Productivity Tools, Simple Presentations and beginning Word Processing	Productivity Program commonalities	Observational Scoring Rubrics
March	Problem Solving & Decision Making Tools, Mind Maps	Visual manipulation of data using object oriented concepts	Observational Scoring Rubrics
April	Visual/Audio Presentations (assisted)	Sound and image manipulation	Observational Scoring Rubrics
May/June	Visual/Audio Presentations (assisted) Research Tools	Presentation tool use	Observational Scoring Rubrics

Pacing Guide 2nd Grade Technology			
	Topics	**Skills/Knowledge**	**Assessment Strategy**
August	Basic Operations and Concepts, Log On/Off, Lab rules	Basic input devices Classroom rules	Observational Scoring Rubrics
September	Keyboarding	Common menu items	Observational

			Scoring Rubrics
October	Productivity Tools, Graphics	Basic drawing tool box items	Observational Scoring Rubrics
November	Social, Ethical, and Human Issues	Social responsibilities	Observational Scoring Rubrics
December	Social, Ethical, and Human Issues	Social responsibilities	Observational Scoring Rubrics
January	Social, Ethical, and Human Issues	Social responsibilities	Observational Scoring Rubrics
February	Productivity Tools, Simple Presentations and beginning Word Processing	Productivity Program commonalities	Observational Scoring Rubrics
March	Problem Solving & Decision Making Tools, Mind Maps	Visual manipulation of data using object oriented concepts	Observational Scoring Rubrics
April	Visual/Audio Presentations (assisted)	Sound and image manipulation	Observational Scoring Rubrics
May/June	Visual/Audio Presentations (assisted) Research Tools	Presentation tool use	Observational Scoring Rubrics

Reinforcing English or Any Other Language

Learning to speak is a skill that sometimes is not emphasized enough in international schools. In schools where the language of instruction is not that of the host country, students spend as little as 3% of the school year speaking the language of instruction. This is far too little in order to help students become fluent speakers.

With the use of a multitude of free voice recording software, students can easily dictate work that they already have written in order to practice their speaking skills. In addition reading ones work aloud is one of the best ways to proofread work during the edit and revise stage of the writing process.

Once students have a finished piece of writing, have them dictate their work and record it for later publication in a digital portfolio. Parents and students alike enjoy and take pride in listening to the improvement in speaking skills over a period of time, which the oral presentations can deliver.

Rubrics

General Grading Rubric

Below is a general grading rubric which can be used for all projects. Most projects especially skill based projects don't always need a precise rubric. However, this rubric can be made more specific to include skills or objects that need to be addressed.

Grade	Student is unable to start or continue without direct instruction. Little to no evidence of understanding of concept(s). Takes a reclusive role in task.	Occasionally needs instruction to finish task. Evidence that student is starting to grasp concept(s). Takes an passive role in task.	Clear and easy to understand all required tasks are fulfilled. Able to convey understanding of concept(s). Takes an passive role in task.	Elaborated or added personal connections or elements that go above and beyond required task. Full understanding of concept(s) and able to elaborate. Takes an active role in task.
K-2	I don't understand and need help. I didn't asked questions and did not help others.	I need help to start or finish. I asked questions or helped others.	I can do it by myself. I helped a friend or asked questions.	I can do it by myself, and I did more than the teacher asked me to do. I helped a friend and asked questions.
3-5	I don't understand and need help throughout the project. I didn't asked questions and did not help others.	I don't understand and need help on what to do in order to finish task. I asked questions or helped others.	I can do it by myself, but may need some help. I asked questions or helped others.	I can do it by myself. I understand the concepts, and I did more than the teacher asked of me to do. I asked questions and helped others.

Specific Rubric Examples

Grade K Drawing Rubric

Standard & Benchmark	Concerned	Approaching	Proficient	Excels
Creativity and Innovation, Students demonstrate creative thinking, construct knowledge, and develop innovative products and processes using technology *create original works as a means of personal or group expression* *ISTE's NETS*	Needs continual assistance to use appropriate tools to create topic image.	Needs occasional assistance to use appropriate tools to create topic image.	Uses appropriate tools to create topic image without additional assistance.	Is able to enhance image by using additional tools not specified or uses tools to create elements of image beyond what was specified.
Technology Operations and Concepts, Students demonstrate a sound understanding of technology concepts, systems, and operations.	Needs continual assistance to start and stop daily system routine.	Needs occasional assistance to start and stop daily system routine.	Is able to start and stop daily system routine without	Is able to start and stop daily system routine without guidance and show evidence of system familiarity.

select and use applications effectively and productively *ISTE's NETS			guidance.	

Grade 1 Drawing Rubric

Standard & Benchmark	Concerned	Approaching	Proficient	Excels
Creativity and Innovation, Students demonstrate creative thinking, construct knowledge, and develop innovative products and processes using technology *create original works as a means of personal or group expression *ISTE's NETS*	Needs continual assistance to use appropriate tools to create topic image.	Needs occasional assistance to use appropriate tools to create topic image.	Uses appropriate tools to create topic image without additional assistance.	Is able to enhance image by using additional tools not specified or uses tools to create elements of image beyond what was specified.
Technology Operations and Concepts, Students demonstrate a sound understanding of technology concepts, systems, and operations. *select and use applications effectively and productively *ISTE's NETS*	Needs continual assistance to start and stop daily system routine.	Needs occasional assistance to start and stop daily system routine.	Is able to start and stop daily system routine without guidance.	Is able to start and stop daily system routine without guidance and show evidence of system familiarity.

Grade 2 Email Rubric

Standard & Benchmark	Concerned	Approaching	Proficient	Excels
Communication and Collaboration, Students use digital media and environments to communicate and work collaboratively, including at a distance, to support individual learning and contribute to the learning of others. *communicate information and ideas effectively to multiple audiences using a variety of media and formats*	Needs continual assistance to create and send email message using friendly letter format.	Needs occasional assistance to create and send email message using friendly letter format.	Is able to create and send email message using friendly letter format without any assistance.	Is able to send email message using friendly letter format and elaborates or shows exceptional familiarity with email system.

*ISTE's NETS				
Technology Operations and Concepts, Students demonstrate a sound understanding of technology concepts, systems, and operations. *select and use applications effectively and productively* *ISTE's NETS*	Needs continual assistance to start and stop daily system routine.	Needs occasional assistance to start and stop daily system routine.	Is able to start and stop daily system routine without guidance.	Is able to start and stop daily system routine without guidance and show evidence of system familiarity.

Below are some suggested basic ideas and rubrics to help you assess the Information Literacy *ISTE's NETS benchmarks. I purposely left the rubrics very basic to give each of you a wider berth in how you teach the skills. Please list specifics within your lesson plan, and feel free to make any changes as you see fit to the information listed below.

Communication and Collaboration

Goal: Have students use technology to communicate/collaborate using local or online Web 2.0 programs.

Target Objectives: Friendly Letter Format, inclusion of subject line, ability to find email address, and CC additional person.

Standard & Benchmark	Concerned	Approaching	Proficient	Excels
Students use digital media and environments to communicate and work collaboratively, including at a distance, to support individual learning and contribute to the learning of others. **communicate information and ideas effectively to multiple audiences using a variety of media and formats** ***ISTE's NETS**	Needs continual assistance to create and send email message using friendly letter format.	Needs occasional assistance to create and send email message using friendly letter format.	Is able to create and send email message using friendly letter format without any assistance.	Is able to send email message using friendly letter format and elaborates or shows exceptional familiarity with email program.

Technology Operations and Concepts

Goal: Observe students using common user interface i.e. Keyboarding/Basic Operations

Target Objectives:
Keyboarding – ability to type without looking at keys, maintain home row, types close to WPM for grade level,

finger placement.
Basic Operations – able to logon/off, open/close programs. Ability to find tools on navigation/toolbar. Can save to private and shared network drives.

Standard & Benchmark	Concerned	Approaching	Proficient	Excels
Students demonstrate a sound understanding of technology concepts, systems, and operations. **select and use applications effectively and productively** *ISTE's NETS	Needs continual assistance to start and stop daily system routine.	Needs occasional assistance to start and stop daily system routine.	Is able to start and stop daily system routine without guidance.	Is able to start and stop daily system routine without guidance and show evidence of system familiarity.

Digital Citizenship

Goal: Students follow computer safety and ethic, as well as computer lab and usage rules.

Target Objectives: handles computer with care, maintains safe working area for hardware, maintains quiet and orderly working environment for self and others.

Standard & Benchmark	Concerned	Approaching	Proficient	Excels
Students understand human, cultural, and societal issues related to technology and practice legal and ethical behavior. **exhibit a positive attitude toward using technology that supports collaboration, learning, and productivity** *ISTE's NETS	Needs constant prompting to maintain safe and/or orderly working environment.	Needs occasional prompting to maintain safe, and orderly working environment.	Maintains a safe and orderly working environment.	Maintains a safe and orderly working environment and helps others.

Creativity and Innovation

Goal: Students use online/offline productivity tools to produce new works.

Target Objectives: Uses productivity software for all or part of writing process.

Standard & Benchmark	Concerned	Approaching	Proficient	Excels
Students demonstrate creative thinking, construct knowledge, and develop innovative products and processes using technology **create original works as a means of**	Needs constant assistance to use productivity tools for writing process.	Needs occasional guidance to use productivity tools for writing process.	Is able to use productivity tools in writing process.	Student shows exceptional familiarity with

personal or group expression *ISTE's NETS				productivity tools.

Research and Information Fluency

Goal: Can use research tools/skills to locate information

Target Objectives: Uses targeted key phrases, uses correct spelling or can use suggested corrected spelling.

Standard & Benchmark	Concerned	Approaching	Proficient	Excels
Students apply digital tools to gather, evaluate, and use information. **locate, organize, analyze, evaluate, synthesize, and ethically use information from a variety of sources and media** ***ISTE's NETS**				

Scope & Sequence

	K	1	2	3	4	5
Computer Expectations • **Digital Citizenship**	K	1	2	3	4	5
Computer Fundamentals • **Technology Operations and Concepts**	K	1	2	3	4	5
Presentation Software • **Creativity and Innovation** • **Communication and Collaboration**	K*	1	2	3	4	5
Introduction to Keyboards & Mouse • **Technology Operations and Concepts**	K	1				
Beginning Graphics • **Creativity and Innovation** • **Communication and Collaboration**	K	1	2			
Visual Mapping Basics *Kidspiration* • **Critical Thinking, Problem Solving, and Decision Making** • **Communication and Collaboration**	K	1	2			

	K	1	2	3	4	5
Researching Skills • **Research and Information Fluency** • **Digital Citizenship**	K	1	2	3	4	5
Keyboarding • **Technology Operations and Concepts**	K	1	2	3	4	5
Web Browsing • **Technology Operations and Concepts** • **Research and Information Fluency**	K	1	2	3	4	5
Word Processing Basics • **Technology Operations and Concepts** • **Communication and Collaboration**		1	2			
Email Basics • **Communication and Collaboration** • **Digital Citizenship**			2	3	4	5
Presentation Basics • **Creativity and Innovation** • **Communication and Collaboration** • **Technology Operations and Concepts**			2	3	4	5
Visual Mapping *Inspiration* • **Critical Thinking, Problem Solving, and Decision Making** • **Communication and Collaboration**				3	4	5
Word Processing • **Creativity and Innovation** • **Technology Operations and Concepts** • **Communication and Collaboration**				3	4	5
Online Collaboration • **Communication and Collaboration** • **Digital Citizenship**				3	4	5
Spreadsheet Basics • **Creativity and Innovation** • **Technology Operations and Concepts**				3	4	5
Spreadsheet Graphing • **Creativity and Innovation** • **Communication and Collaboration**				3	4	5
Spreadsheet Formulas					4	5
Basic HTML • **Creativity and Innovation** • **Communication and Collaboration**						5

Score Sheet

In theory, every task should have some type of <u>score sheet</u> used to inform parents and the student how they did on the assignment. The score sheet should be returned to the student attached to the assignment material as soon as possible. This helps the student know where they stand in understanding the subject matter. Parents will also be grateful for the immediate feedback concerning their child. transparency is key to running any program. Below is a score sheet that I use in my technology classes. The score sheet doesn't have to be elaborate.

Score Sheet Example

Lesson Title *Google Earth 3*

Overview: Google Earth is an important learning tool that is used across multiple subject areas. With Location Aware applications becoming the norm, Google Earth is becoming ever more important.

Goal: Students will apply user interface skills learned, by exploring that basic usage of Google Earth.

Rubric

Concerned (1)	Approaching (2)	Proficient (3)	Excels (4)
Student is unable to start or continue without direct instruction. Little to no evidence of understanding of concept(s).	Occasionally needs instruction to finish task. Evidence that student is starting to grasp concept(s).	Clear and easy to understand all required tasks are fulfilled. Able to convey understanding of concept(s).	Elaborated or added personal connections or elements that go above and beyond required task. Full understanding of concept(s) and able to elaborate.

Benchmarks

11) Research and Information Fluency, Students apply digital tools to gather, evaluate, and use information.. evaluate and select information sources and digital tools based on the appropriateness to specific tasks	
15) Critical Thinking, Problem Solving, and Decision Making, Students use critical thinking skills to plan and conduct research, manage projects, solve problems, and make informed decisions using appropriate digital tools and resources.. collect and analyze data to identify solutions and/or make informed decisions	
18) Digital Citizenship, Students understand human, cultural, and societal issues related to technology and practice legal and ethical behavior.. exhibit a positive attitude toward using technology that supports collaboration, learning, and productivity	
24) Technology Operations and Concepts, Students demonstrate a sound understanding of technology concepts, systems, and operations.. understand and use	

technology systems	

Standards & Benchmarks

The following SIX standards are derived from the ISTE's National Educational Technology Standards.

Operations and Concepts

Students will use electronic devices effectively and productively.
Routine usage, such as keyboarding and learning common features in program user interfaces, leads to ease of use which transfers to others systems and applications.
Keyboarding, Email, Office Suites
(Kindergarten)
vocabulary (mouse, keyboard, monitor, icon, button, cursor, dock, pull-down menu, log-out)
(Grades 1-2)
vocabulary (homerow, CPU, printer, toolbar, menu, window, folder, program)
(Grades 3-5)
vocabulary (storage device, application, scanner, digitize, network, Internet, server, workstation, HTML)

Creativity and Innovation

Students construct innovative products using technology.
Using a topic in class, have students publish their work, such as a video, sound, document with graphs, or slide show.
Movie Maker, iMovie, Audacity

Communication and Collaboration

Students use digital media and environments to communicate and work collaboratively.
Use collaborative office suite to have students work together on projects. This can include communication programs such as email or voice tools to discuss project details and ideas.
Wiki, Zoho, Google Docs, Skype, Email

Research and Information Fluency

Students apply digital tools to gather, evaluate, and use information.
Use online search engine, directories, or websites to research for project in class. Proper search techniques as well as citation are part of this standard.
Google, Yahoo, MSN Live

Critical Thinking, Problem Solving, and Decision Making

Students manage projects, solve problems, and make informed decisions using appropriate digital tools and resources.
Organizational software or mind mapping software can easily be integrated into any project to help students manage the workflow and ideas.
Freemind, Kidspiration, Excel

Digital Citizenship

Students understand and practice legal and ethical behavior while using technological devices.
Appropriate use of technology can be integrated into school wide behavior and social constructivist themes.
ESLRS & PALS, Current Classroom Social Problems

Yearlong Guide

As a guide to how to plan out a year for younger grade levels with dedicated technology time, try breaking the year into a basic operations and behavior section followed by a Internet safety course and follow up with project based learning.

The three step process is a method that ensures that students are guided and have enough opportunities to master skills. In additions it is a perfect way to differentiate learning in the classroom.
- Step 1: Introduce concepts to class. Have a very structured lessons with lots of guidance.
- Step 2: Re-Teach the skills and concepts using guidance, but allowing those who understand to go ahead and or help fellow classmates.
- Step 3: Once again have students use the skills and concepts to create and elaborate using the same tools as before.

Basic Operations & Classroom Management	Students will need to know the expectations of using technology. Also, time is needed to teach students the ins and outs of using the varied technology resources from computers to handheld devices.
CyberSMART or NetSMART Curriculum	Use an Internet safety curriculum to teach the basics of safety, manners, and proper behavior while online.
Introduction to Applications	Teach students using a **three step process** how to use key applications used for content creation.
Classroom Collaboration Projects	Work with homeroom teachers to integrate their curriculum or learning objectives into a project using the applications taught during technology time.

Digital Native Myth

A major misconception being perpetrated throughout news media is that young child to adults are in tune with technology and they are experts when it comes to anything technology related. It is true that you people have a knack for certain technologies be it a cell phone, Wii, or the Facebook interface. What I have found teaching students of every grade level from Kindergarten to Seniors is that they may have a superficial know-how, but they really are not trained or have in depth knowledge of the main aspects of technology such as logic, user-interfaces, or basic researching skills. I was appalled at the lack of the skill sets of most students when ever I first arrive at a school.

For this reason this is why it is critical that teachers spend the time to teach the basic skills that students will need in the workforce and in a higher education setting. Skills such as sound researching, online collaboration, online etiquette, and using computers for logic manipulation are just some of the skills that will need to be taught and reinforced in order to ensure that students are prepared.
Reference: Northwestern University, Digital Nativism Digital Delusions and Digital Deprivation

Digital Portfolios

Just as with teacher web sites Digital portfolios should be a very flexible. With students potentially moving from school to school, their achievements should be able to move with them. Each classroom teacher may also have different requirements for how the portfolio should be made and what it should contain.

Issues
- **portability**, changing of schools: Choosing a program be it static or dynamic, should be portable especially for international students.
- **audience**: Portfolios should be made in a manner that targets a specific audience. As students move through grade levels, the audience will change ending in a portfolio to help students enter a post secondary institution.
- **media**: uploads, attachments
- **privacy**: Insuring that only a targeted audience should be paramount especially for younger students.
- **collaboration, blog versus journal format**: The type of format chosen should reflect the function of the portfolio.

ESL Support

Technology can play a big part in supporting ESL students. Mobile devices have freed students and teachers so they no longer are restricted to the classroom or lab when using ESL support software or hardware.

Portable Media Devices

Be it an Apple product or any other device, many devices have translator programs that students can use anywhere. Using such a device allows students to write questions or answer a teacher if they need assistance due to a lack of language ability. Using a translator will not be very useful if a student's doesn't already have a command of their native language.

Laptop or Desktop Computer

Having a web page open to a web based translator program is very useful if a student already has a command of their native language. Having one computer dedicated for a translator is an easy way to help ESL students in class.

Integrate Technology

` Since hardware and software are constantly evolving, listing lessons with specific software or hardware to use is a never ending struggle. Instead listed below are technology integration ideas that are general enough that one can search online for the specific tools needed but the overall idea is enough to get one started. Ask your Technology Integrationist if they can help implement any of the following ideas.

Even mundane or simple tasks can incorporate technology adding to the learning experience. No matter how routine the task may seem adding technology can add to the experience adding new life to the task.

Focus

Targeted Content
- Use TeacherTube for resources then have students reflect.
- Use WebQuest for pre-made online lesson about content matter.

Collaboration
- Use an online office suite that will allow your students to work in real time on the same document. **Any subject matter** can be reflected upon using this method.
- Use an online collaboration tool to have students dialog with each other, or reflect.

Math Skills
- Use an online multiplayer game to use competition to motivate students to learn their math facts.
- Use spreadsheet software to create graphs.
- Use of consumption sites such as IXL and Kahn Academy

Field Trips or Outside Classroom
- Use devices such as cameras, cell phones, or personal media devices to capture images, sounds, and to take notes for use with presentations software for playback later. If the devices are location aware, they can plot the points using Google Earth or other programs that use GPS.

Reading
- Use Google Earth to map locations mentioned in a book. Then create a presentation using Google Earth's playback feature, where narration and addition written information can be added to enhance the presentation.

Presentations
- Use any office suite to create a presentation on **any subject matter** studied in class that can be played back later. Some online based presentation programs can be viewed 24/7 from anywhere in the world.

WebQuests
- Use pre-made WebQuests to utilize online content, or have students make their own WebQuest!

Movie Creation
- Use any movie program along with the writing process to create a movie on any subject matter.

Digital Media
- Use graphics programs to create images which can be used to teach skills, or in conjunction with written or oral presentation.

Word Processing
- Using any word processor is a great way to have students practice their typing skills and how to practice

a skill that they will often need to use.

Research
- Basic researching skill can be used for any project. Finding or teaching how to find appropriately leveled resources online should be the emphasis.

Mind Mapping
- Using a mind map for any project that can be planned out. Any subject matter can use the benefit of planning out using a mind map.

Objective

Teaching students how to use specific programs or hardware is not what teaching technology is about. Rather it is about teaching students the Art of Computer Use. This involves fostering a child's innate ingenuity to adapt to different programs and hardware using the basic skills and familiarization of all the aspects of technology they have already encountered and might encounter. This will allow students to spend time using technology in a higher level, as opposed to mundane usage of skills that will become out-of-date, by creating meaningful projects. This in turn prepares students for additional projects in the homeroom class where teachers can spend time concentrating on teaching content versus the mundane task of teaching basic technology usage. In addition, students are to learn proper online safety skills and manners, which is becoming evermore important in a world where a personal presence online is now common place.

A major component of technology that must be on the front burner for all technology integrationists is the importance of awareness on the Internet. From cyberbullying to exposing every aspect of ones life online, teaching students to be aware of what is placed online for all to see is a big unknown. No one knows how or what this information will be used by companies, governments, or friends other than the obvious marketing and socializing. Teaching students to be prudent starting with the youngest technology users will not hurt.

The goal of an integrationist should be to promote and help in the instruction of all aspects of proven technology. That is to say not to potentially waste precious classroom time on unproven technologies. In addition, one of the most important aspects is to not interfere with the core curriculum taught in the classroom. Often integrationists can be overzealous and impose their agenda on classroom teachers, which can hamper the core curriculum being taught. It is a fine line that must be taken in order to promote yet not interfere with what is being taught.

Big Three Technology Skill Areas
1. Digital Citizenship, Skills include cyberbullying and personal safety.
2. Research, Skills include online resource evaluation and search techniques.
3. Creative Productivity, Skills include critical thinking and millennia learning techniques.

Goal
Every school will have a different expectation as to what role technology plays in a school's curriculum. If technology is to be taught as a subject even in a collaborative environment, the goal should be to have projects that cover all the different NETS standards. This really can only be achieved if a school's policy mandated that teachers report on technology standards and benchmarks. Whether the homeroom teacher or the technology integrationist reports doesn't really matter as long as someone if clearly responsible.

Consumption Versus Production
Specialists should help students and teachers find both consumption and production uses of technology. A consumption use would include using ready made web sites for core curriculum skills development and review,

such as a math testing, review, or instruction site. While production skills such as using hardware and software resources to create new material such as a movie, written work, or robot. Often technology might fulfill both roles. Using technology as a consumption tool where it is used for communication while also using it for creating a product would cover both roles.

Content Versus Skills

Specialist are often thought of by administration and homeroom teachers as teaching or supporting only technology skills. Specialist however often think as themselves as teaching both skills and subject relevant content. The content aspect is the part that often causes problems in regards to collaboration or scheduling issues. If the administration or curriculum coordinator thinks of specialists as only teaching skills, then the specialist's role will be very basic and essentially just a support role. The ideal situation will have the school's policy for specialists to teach both skills and content. The idea of teaching both hand in hand will be a critical issue and will play itself out in meetings with individual teachers and grade level planning times. If the teachers do not see the specialist as a teaching content and skills then problems can arise.

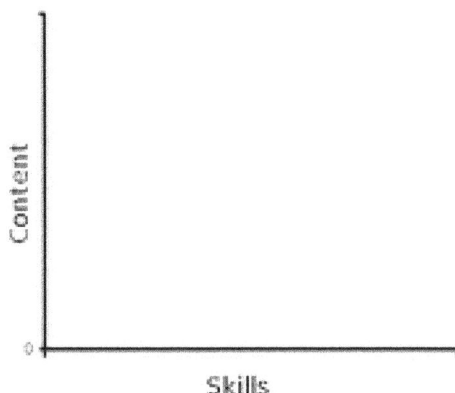

For Physical education teacher the content might include the health aspects of the subject. For art teachers it might include the history of art. For technology teachers the content could include the 21st Century knowledge, programming, or researching fundamentals. Regardless, technology specialists should aim for both skills and content for every lesson.

Streamline Versus Experimentation

Creating projects that clearly fall in line with the curriculum will ensure that students are following a scope and sequence of technology skills as well as fulfilling core subject standards and benchmarks. However, experimentation should not be completely ruled out as technology is constantly in a state of change and new and exciting new programs and hardware are being introduced. Teachers should be encouraged to try new things, but to use tried and true software and hardware as well.

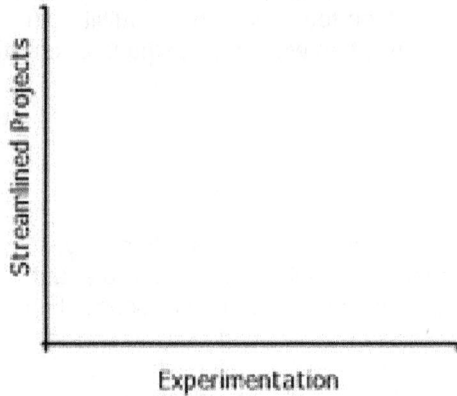

Y-axis: Streamlined Projects
X-axis: Experimentation

Individual Versus Collaboration

Teachers are often asked to work collaboratively with each other. This is not always an easy request to fill for many reasons. One major hurdle is the uncertainty of the skill level of the team members or the reliability of the resources used. A good mix of classroom only projects where one works only with themselves should be encouraged. Sometimes a teacher needs to see for themselves if a projects is worthy or they might just want to differentiate their instruction or focus on something more than other teachers in their group.

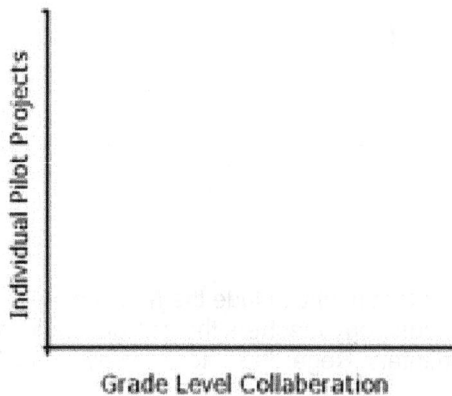

Y-axis: Individual Pilot Projects
X-axis: Grade Level Collaberation

Simple Versus Complex

Many technology skills can be considered basic, and are often referred to as Basic Operations. These skills are vital and often not taught properly. If the students come into a class unsure of how to do basic technology related skills, this will cause an inconvenience for the homeroom teachers since they will have to stop instruction to bring all students up to speed. Using the year to increase the basic operations skills as well as including projects to encourage students to use higher learning skills such as analyzing and synthesis should be encouraged.

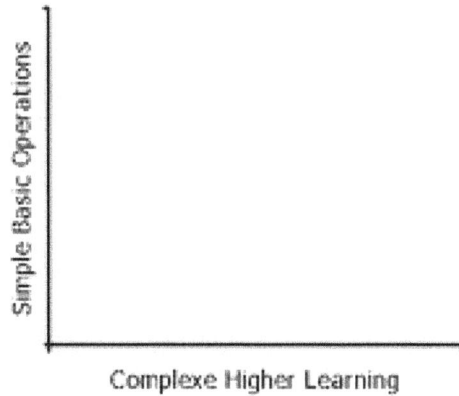

Y-axis: Simple Basic Operations
X-axis: Complexe Higher Learning

Age of Exploration

Gone should be the days of using technology as a gimmick or haphazardly using technology in the classroom. The last couple of decades teachers used technology with little consideration other than it was new and exciting. thinking of a purpose after the fact is not what teachers are supposed to do. Unfortunately too often teachers revert back to exploration and not using technology to enhance their core subject matter. Planning is key to ensure that the use of technology is thoughtful and meaningful. However, the collaborative aspect of integration is often the most difficult to achieve.

Technology should be thought of as a foundation, balancing the scale of overarching social aspects and technology as a learning tool for the core subjects.

What should be avoided with careful diplomacy is using technology as a marketing tool by administrations who promote a school's superiority by bell and whistle projects that showcase the use of the latest technological hardware and software with minimal longevity in regards to higher learning.

Computer Fundamentals

All students should have the basic PC fundamentals, which include Word Processing, Number, and Presentation software skills. With these three programs teachers do not have to spend precious time teaching basic computer skills, but rather can target their time teaching content.

In addition I would add Research to the basic skills, but these can also be taught by homeroom teachers as it is not solely a technology skill.

ESL Practice

Giving the opportunity for ESL students to practice a target language is often a difficult task. Students have many apprehensions when it comes to speaking their non-native tongue aloud. Technology can play a vital role in helping ESL students by providing another opportunity to practice speaking aloud.

Having a writing or drawing aspect of every project, will supply multiple opportunities for a spoken component to projects. Using programs such as Audacity or Garageband are fun and easy ways for students to record their speaking. It also is a personal activity where students can dell comfortable as they will not be speaking in front of their peers. Also, by having them review their speaking they can notice their writing mistakes more easily as audible mistakes are more pronounced.

Integrationist Role

There are two schools of thought on the role of an integrationist. On one hand is the Integrationist who solely helps train teachers in the art of technology use. On the other is the specialist who teaches technology directly to students usually in a block class format. Just as with any two extremes the best choice usually lies somewhere in between.

The Pure Integrationist

The problem with the integrationist who only works with training teachers is the impracticality of the job. Many teachers are extremely busy and can't find the time, or they are apprehensive to use technology, even after being trained and will revert to non-technological methods. The only guarantee for teachers to fully embrace this model is to make it a mandate from administration. This raises the problem of teacher buy-in. Just as with students, our goal should be to achieve a high level of motivation, and directives never will suffice. This also can lead to a student population where not every child has been taught or exposed to critical technology skills, which can hamper them in coming years.

The Pure Specialist

The problem with a specialist role where the integrationist only works with students is that teachers never fully become comfortable with technology and never expand on the skills that the students learn for a more holistic approach. In addition, the integrationist can be burdened with a great deal of teaching and potential assessments, leading to an inequitable and inefficient work load.

The Ideal Solution

The ideal solution would be a compromise between the two extremes, where the integrationist gives a basic coverage of critical technology skills to ensure coverage of key concepts given by a true experienced expert, not a teacher who has a vague understanding. Also, they train teachers so they are confident in their own abilities, and to work on collaborative projects. This will allow for a more achievable workload for the integrationist as well as to create an atmosphere where teachers can at their own pace gain the skills needed to branch out on their own.

Examples

Examples of Problems of the Pure Integrationist & Specialists
- inherent over reliance of teacher's ability to teach technology skills. Not all teachers are comfortable or have the ability to introduce key concepts. An experience technology integrationist would make a better choice.
- Often integrationists promote online resources as a method for teaching technology, such as link lists and online videos. This is essentially a direct or rote instruction method, which is a very low level teaching method and should not be used.
- Depending on teachers to guarantee that students are taught key concepts throughout their schooling is wishful thinking at best. Most teachers run a hectic schedule and barely have time to get their core curriculum done in a typical school year. This leads to a student population where some students understand grade level concepts while others do not.
- Specialists are typically not available to help train teachers due to workload. In addition, they have a more difficult time integrating core curriculum with technology leading to a lack of project based learning opportunities.

Examples of Benefits of the Integrationist Specialist Merged Role
- Experts can lead instruction in the classroom while teachers take a passive role. Some concepts don't even need the teacher to be present if it is not tied into the classroom curriculum.
- Experts can co-teach after students are taught concepts, allowing for more hand holding for students who have not reached a proficient level. This also allows for classroom curriculum to move ahead while

using the technology concepts learned.
- Experts can provide a support role once concepts are mostly underway in the classroom. The teacher can concentrate on curriculum while also having been exposed to technology concepts. This gives the teacher a working knowledge of the capabilities of the concepts taught and the general students capability using the concepts.

K-12 Strategy

With the many years of experience that I, and my good friend and co-work Tim Bray, have in the field I believe the best strategy for integrating technology is simple and easy to implement. It is a hybrid system of blocked classes along with a traditional integrationist role of helping teachers in many different aspects.

- Pre-K
  - Teacher led simple use of technology. Using tablets and basic software to support learning in the classroom. Having a few devices for center use is ideal in addition a computer lab or laptop carts can be used as well. Keeping the use very simple is ideal and there typically is no need for blocked classes, other than the occasional help from an integrationist.
- Kindergarten - 2nd Grade
  - Block Classes. It is critical to have blocked classes usually once per week in order to get through the basics needed for students to have the background knowledge to use computers effectively. Teachers also will find it useful to have students trained in the basics so when classroom projects that utilize technology are done, they are easier to instruct. They will often still need assistance from an integrationist.
- 3rd - 5th Grade
  - Integrationist. With a solid foundation given in the K-2 grades, most instruction can be given be homeroom teachers. Occasionally an integrationist may need to give a refresher course or give instruction for a new topic. An integrationist may have one of three roles for this range of grades.
- 6th Grade (transition year)
  - Mandatory Elective on Familiarization of School used software and hardware. Often new students may not have the background knowledge and skills necessary to work on projects with other classmates. This is an unnecessary burden for teachers and may cause the class to slow its pace and take more time than planned. This negatively impacts students learning. Having a mandatory class for new incoming students will ensure a minimum set of skills that teachers know all students will have. This class should be at the beginning of the school year.
- 7th - 8th Grade
  - Mandatory Advisory Units on Cyberbullying and Social Issues. Middle school students for the most part are just learning about themselves and their classmates on many different levels. Socialization is a major part of their lives during this time period and technology can play a big part in their lives both positively and negatively. Having students take mandatory units on Cyberbullying is critical at this stage. The units can be given at any time of the year to help in coincide with any school-wide initiatives being done by the counseling department.
  - Specialized electives on technology use with constructivist emphasis. Offering more in depth courses for specific areas of technology should be offered for those students interested in technology. Having time for students to start exploring their interests is crucial at this stage if they are to gain enough background knowledge and skills to compete with other students for coveted entrance positions at the University level.
- 9th Grade (transition year)
  - Mandatory Elective on Familiarization of School used software and hardware. Often new students may not have the background knowledge and skills necessary to work on projects with other classmates. This is an unnecessary burden for teachers and may cause the class to slow its pace and take more time than planned. This negatively impacts students learning. Having a mandatory class for new incoming students will ensure a minimum set of skills that teachers

know all students will have. This class should be at the beginning of the school year.
- 10th - 12th Grades
  - Mandatory Advisory Units on the impact of technology on their lives. High school students are still coming into their own selves and understanding of their actions on themselves and those around them. Socialization is still a major part of their lives during this time period and technology can play a big part both positively and negatively. Having students take mandatory units on the impact of technology around them is critical at this stage. The units can be given at any time of the year to help in coincide with any school-wide initiatives being done by the counseling department.
  - Specialized electives on technology use with constructivist emphasis. Offering more in depth courses for specific areas of technology should be offered for those students interested in technology. Having time for students to explore and refine their interests is crucial at this stage if they are to gain enough background knowledge and skills to compete with other students for coveted entrance positions at the University level.

Showcasing

I thought that some of you might be interested in creating a project where students showcase an image, and or their writing. Using Voicethread for this purpose is a great idea as it also incorporates voice allowing students to practice their speaking skills. In addition, students can get feedback from others, instead of just their parents and the teacher, creating a sense of real world meaning.

Here is a web page with many examples of leveled projects, http://voicethread4education.wikispaces.com/K-2

Technology Misunderstood

Too often I have witnessed technology being used for the wrong reason. School administrators may at heart have good reasons for implementing technology such as one to one laptop programs, or mobile lab usage, but more often they only use technology as a marketing ploy for enrollment. We are in an era where the adults in charge have no idea of the potential emotional threats that are children are in when we allow free unfettered access to the Internet or to particular software. I once had an administrator, while working in a school in China, tell me that all children are innocent and would never go to sites containing adult content, and if they did we would deal with it after the fact. What I was thinking to myself was after the emotional damage was done. When we give students a gun or a car we train them to use those tools with extreme caution, and we as teachers and administrators should do the same with technology.

We need to insure that children get trained on proper use of technology throughout their schooling, not just in elementary and high school. Also, parents need training as well on what the dangers are and how to insure that their children can be safeguarded.

Tenants

Here are the basic important aspects of technology integration that should be included in all lessons regarding technology.

Lessons or Units should...
- include an **inquiry based aspect** utilizing some form of digital research skills, may not necessarily need to use digital resource. Encouraging students to connect ideas and thoughts into a higher level of

cognitive inquiry makes for a more well rounded student and thought provoking classroom.

- follow **blended learning** model, allowing for class-time to be used for one on one instruction and overall differentiated learning for all. Change the traditional pedagogy of teachers will not be easy, but with the added benefit of freeing up class time to help or enrich students personally will help target more directly our efforts.
- include **modular technology aspects**, allowing for easy overall differentiated learning for students, and incorporation flexibility. Creating modules that can plug into any lesson at any time of the year will help motivate teachers to use technology.
- use only a **few unique key concepts** per year to keep the learning curve manageable, and to ensure that they are repeated in order to refine the skill or knowledge. Oftentimes one time only or brief overviews can lead to lost hopelessness or lack of true understand of the potential uses. Transferable knowledge is the most important aspect of technology use.
- address the **social implications** of its use. No matter how small a potential problem may be it is our responsibility to make sure students understand potential problems that may arise.
- focus **not on specific company ecosystems**, but on general themes that run across all systems. This will help students transition and adapt to any system they may encounter in the future.

Parent Focus

Habits
Parent involvement is very important in the early stages of a child's introduction to technology. Safety is often the main concern, but good habits also play an import part.

Parent Workshops

Having knowledge of what is being taught in class and reinforcing the concepts will help instill habits that will safely carry your child throughout their school career and beyond. Offering Parent workshops every week is a great way to help train parents and introduce concepts of important skills used in the classroom.

"Thanks for your enthusiastic effort in educating the moms! We really appreciate it! We are using the Google Docs skills you showed us in planning the Xmas Party - revision history, real time chat.... ^^ Thank you!" -Pik Kwan

"I wanted to thank you for the computer workshop I took from you last year - it just saved us from losing $800! We advertised a boat on Craigslist and got a response from a fraudulent buyer. Luckily the information you gave me in the workshop helped to make me aware of possible phishing and other scams and I took measures to make sure the emails from Paypal were real (they weren't!)." -Rick Jones

Newsletters
Every new unit of study will have a newsletter explaining the concepts and what a parent can do to help instill important new skills.

Newsletters are a perfect way to keep parents informed. They are also a way to extend your instruction especially for hard to learn topics. Remember that many parents may not have technology skills themselves, so using an print copy of what takes place in a classroom is still an important function in today's world.

Parent Common Concerns

In every school parents will have concerns about how technology is used in the classroom. All these questions can be addressed in the classroom, where students are taught directly about the concerns. Also, Parents can be given opportunities to learn how to deal with their concerns by attending workshops. Below are some common concerns of parents that are addressed in the Parent Workshops,

- Playing games
- Preventing viewing of adult content
- Cyberbullying
- Privacy
- Home supervision
- Online social skills

Parent involvement is very important in the early stages of a child's introduction to technology. Safety is often the main concern, but establishing good habits also plays an import part.

Vacation Extracurricular

Here are some ideas that can help your child continue their learning over vacation time, while still having an element of fun included.

Typing Games online are a perfect way for your child to practice their technology skills.
- Dance Mat Typing
- Typing Club

With Tablets including the iPad and Galaxy Tab to name a couple, online apps which tend to be free are another great choice. Both the Apple App and Google Android stores have education sections. The Android apps can even run in a browser on both Apple and Windows computers! Just download Google Chrome on your computer.

Ask Your Child's Teacher

Most teachers have a learning links page of web sites or online resources to help extend the classroom learning experience. These resources are a perfect way to extend your child's learning experience over extended periods of time outside the classroom. If possible ask your child's expected teaching for the following year if they have a learning links page as well to prepare your child for the next year.

Pedagogy

When teaching, using a three step model is what I have found to be the most successful. The three step model works for all grade levels and promotes retention of content and basic skills.

STEP 1

The first step involves demonstrating to students the targeted technology be it hardware, software, or methodology. Having the instruction broken down into digestible chunks over many lessons works well and allows students time to master the steps.

STEP 2

The second step is to have a scripted project where students are allowed to practice the skills needed, but with clear instruction and guidance throughout the whole process.

STEP 3

The final step involves having students apply the knowledge or skill they have learned and practiced in order to create a product or other assessment. Younger students may still need quite a bit of hand holding, but some will be able to apply the knowledge they have learned and apply it. This will also allow the teacher more time to help those who need it more.

Planning Strategy
There are many different types of planning strategies that can be used when planning out units and lessons. From Understanding by Design, modular, and flipped classrooms. Choosing the method that works best for you should be the only factor, unless a particular methodology is mandated by your administration.

Backchannels

Dealing with a teacher's personality in addition to the different learning styles and personalities of students always makes for an interesting mix, and having an additional tool for the classroom can only help. However, teachers need to be trained to use back channels to ensure that they are inclusive and using it properly, by pulling in a back channel commenter into the mainstream discussion. Otherwise it can be a social crutch for those students who normally do not participate in classroom discussions.

Ideas for using technology as a back channel discussion forum. Use Twitter or other social media web site or chat room program to help encourage students to participate in a discussion. Monitor the back channel while keeping the general classroom discussion going. Once a good thread has started in the back channel, include it in the main discussion. This should help the soft spoken or general discussion non-participant to participate.

Tips:
- Make sure everyone has access to the back channel program or site.
- Don't call out the person who makes a back channel comment directly, let them come forward so as to not scare them if they are shy.
- Monitor the back channel often or assign one student to do so, otherwise threads can go by quickly and be missed.
- Go over proper etiquette before using a back channel to avoid improper behavior.

Integrationist Pitfalls

The Problem with Integrationists
A pitfall of the integrationist is the dreaded YouTube support, email list, and inaccessible integrationist. To take a maybe tasteless stab at Apple, calling a program professional development when it is nothing more than links or basis 101 workshops with no connections to curriculum, standards and benchmarks, or wide focus to encompass all solutions to a goal, is similar to Apple's "genius bar". Calling something when it clearly is not does no good, and is perhaps a waste of time. Teachers students and parents should be learning how applications and skills can improve student learning, not teach them how to use one particular thing well with no evident path to integration into curriculum.
- Sending an email with a list of technology resources is not what integrationists should be doing. Instead send one resource and stop by each room to explain in person what was sent out, and whether or not the teacher found it useful.
- The YouTube Solution. Youtube is a great resource. However sending teachers requesting help a link to a YouTube video is, for a lack of a better term, lame. Instead send a YouTube video, but also promptly show up in person to resolve the issue. If you can't make it immediately, ask them to make an appointment. Most teachers can find a backup plan to hold off their problem. It is better to give full service than to send a video that may frustrate them further.
- Being stagnant in an office may make for a centralized location for easy access, but being present in classroom, or doing walk through gives far more insight as to what is going on in the classrooms. In addition, teachers will often ask for advice that they wouldn't get to ask otherwise with their busy

schedules.

Integrationist Priorities

Priorities

The main purpose of being involved with technology in a school setting is to assist in student learning and helping teachers to do their job. Often technology related jobs get caught up in the 80's mentality that technology is about teaching Word or Excel as stand alone subjects without a connection to curriculum content.

The **Golden Rule** for technology Integration is if a student or other non-professional can teach it, then you shouldn't be doing it. A professional integrationist should be using their skills and knowledge for a higher purpose such as strategic planning with teaching staff. A classic example of what an integrationist should not do but happens a lot is when a teacher requests help, they are sent an email with links. A better solution would be to research the solution and stop by and have a discussion with the teacher. Many time teachers are unaware of how a solution can be pieced together with hardware and software solutions. Having a discussion ensures that a proper solution is found, even though it takes more time and effort.

Tech integrationist should abide by the motto "we are here to help serve you."

High Priority
- Overarching curriculum integration for grade level and by subject
- Parent training for social adaptation of technology use.
- Digital citizenship concept integration
- Resource streamlining and organizing for classroom use
- Professional development training for programs or devices specifically requested by teachers.

Low Priority
- Help Desk, fixing printers and other mundane tasks
- Professional development training for programs or devices not requested by teachers. A simple refresher of basic online researching skills and a link reference web page of common places to find online tutorials, such as YouTube, should suffice. Teachers can always ask for help if needed for one on one instruction.
- In-class program training of programs and devices for students
- Resource creation, such as Screencasts or cheat sheets. These can readily be found on the Internet. Don't even waste time creating a resource page, instead teach proper research skills!

Integrationist Roles

When working as an integrationist there are two ways to interact with teachers. One method which is easy is to continually notify teachers by email or other communication method. The problem typically associated with this method is that teachers are typically busy and won't take the time to investigate on their own the links or references supplied. If this method is chosen it would be a good idea to include with each reference some type of synopsis explaining what the references are. The second method is to do a stop by, or short visit in the classroom. This is a perfect method if a few rules are followed, such as keep the visits short, and until a relationship is built keep the topics of discussion light. Using a combination of both of these methods is the best option that will serve the integrationist well.

Blocked Technology Classes

Integrationists, whatever level they work in, should be required to teach a blocked class. There are many benefits including, a school can offer technology courses taught by an expert, if offers a means for other teachers to see technology teaching methods modeled, and it builds a rapport with students.

Professional Development

A major aspect of the integrationists is to train students, teachers, and parents. All three groups must be addressed in order for technology to be successful i a school. Unfortunately most integrationists focus solely on teacher training, with some help of students. The parent group is not of focus of most schools as evident by looking at school web sites and educational technology blogs. The level of service that should be avoided for an integrationist is the YouTube or email list.

NETS Every Year

In order to teach students in a comprehensive manner, every year each of the six different NET's strands should be taught. Each of the strands should have a at least one project each year. The projects should be leveled appropriately and using a creative approach is crucial to insure that subject matter relevant to the classroom subject matter focus is supported.

Often middle school and high school students are left to their own intentions and are expected to learn the use of technology by themselves. This is a disservice to the students as technology is constantly evolving and every students has a different level of exposure to technology. Having a technology curriculum or integration throughout their schooling can only ensure that all students receive the same level of exposure and skill sets.

Steps of Integration

Potential Uses

Teachers need to know basic usage. Focusing on small baby step projects for elementary homeroom teachers is ideal.

Basic Skills

Demonstrate basic usage skills for common applications and hardware.

Higher level Usage and Strategies

The most difficult aspect of an integrationists role is the higher level usage of technology in the classroom. This goes above and beyond just using software and hardware. Mapping of the use of technology throughout the year and projects and how all the skills related to technology are linked together and build on each other.

Integration Strategies

- Walkthroughs, relationship building
- PD, availability of skills and potential of technology
- Block Classes, basic coverage
- Have a technology team, ease of getting the word out to grade and subject levels.

Technology Use Pitfalls

One major concern for technology teachers is how to ensure that students receive a structured and basic skill coverage throughout the grade levels. This is not an issue if the classes are block, but it is if the teachers are in charge of the technology assessments.

Safe Searching

All Google search features (YouTube, Images, Web) has a "strict" search setting that can easily be toggled using the "search settings" in the upper right-hand corner. It only takes a few minutes to have your students set it, and it will limit unexpected search results.

Cyberbullying

When children have unfettered access to the Internet and social media sites, problems often arise. Preventing them from using all of the sites is not an option as they are great tools to be used in the classroom. Finding a safe way to use the online social tools is difficult but can be done.

What to do and how to prevent cyberbullying can be achieved if certain safeguards are taken.

What Parents Can Do

- Teach our children that the Internet is not just a "rules-free" environment of social interaction. In fact, it's a place where many dangers lurk precisely because its "rules-free."
- When there is a cyber-bullying problem, parents should call an attorney, then call the school and put everything in writing.
- If the school won't help, parents can go to court and get a restraining order. Most forms of cyberbullying, and ALL sexual bullying, are covered by civil rights laws, which means a judge can issue orders granting "equitable" relief, such as requiring the school to utilize available technology to stop cyber-activity, or moving the offending student off-campus.
- When schools fail to protect students from cyber-bullying, the Department of Education's Office For Civil Rights has authority to force schools to take action under threat of serious financial sanction and other punishments. The Obama administration claims to have a more dedicated commitment to the prevention of sexual bullying on campus than the Bush administration, but under Obama's leadership, the Department of Education has thus far refused to respond to complaints about the cyber-bullying that caused a near-suicide at Hofstra. Rather than addressing the issue and instructing Hofstra to take effective steps to stop sexual cyber-bullying, Obama's Department of Education ducked the issue on procedural grounds.

What Administrators Can Do

- The US Supreme Court ruled in 1969 that you can sanction cyber-bullying notwithstanding "free speech" concerns, where the conduct "has caused or foreseeably will cause 'interference with the rights of students to be secure'". Tinker, 1969. The federal Third Circuit Court of Appeals stated more succinctly in 2002: "There is no constitutional right to be a bully".
- Any cyber-bullying that impairs a student's ability to participate in education not only can but must be redressed, because federal civil rights laws impose a duty on schools to provide "prompt and effective" relief.
- Federal courts have ruled that schools must act, even if the bullying occurs off-campus, if the bullying:
  - a. is viewed at school
  - b. is posted on a publicly available website at the school
  - c. is the topic of conversation at school
  - d. leads to graffiti at school
  - e. requires faculty attention or on-campus medical/counseling attention
  - f. causes other students to express fear or concern

g.   is evidence indicating a pattern of similar past activity

h.   is related to other disciplinary issues on campus

Student Free Time

Technology is a resource to be used by students to learn while at school. Often the case, some teachers will use technology as a babysitter when there is downtime. The main problem with using technology is often a shared resource. If one teacher uses the resources for non-educational purposes, then other students may lose an opportunity to learn. As a fellow teacher or technology coordinator, try to encourage others to be more structured while using technology. Having a simple list of pre-categorized educational game sites in conjunction of using a checklist is a good way to encourage proper use of the technology resources at your school.

Free Time Slip

Name: _____

Date: _____

Class: _____

Web Site 1

_____

_____ I Learned _____ I Practiced _____

Web Site 2

_____

_____ I Learned _____ I Practiced _____

Name: _____

Date: _____

Class: _____

Web Site 1

_____

_____ I Learned _____ I Practiced _____

Web Site 2

_____

_____ I Learned _____ I Practiced _____

Computer Expectations Presentation

Computer Lab Expectations 1st - 12th Grades

Computer Lab Expectations

Users are responsible for good behavior on the Internet.

GENERAL SCHOOL RULES APPLY!

This includes cell phones, Nintendo, PSP, MP3 players, and other Personal Media Players!

Be Clean
Use Kleenex!
Wash Your Hands

Food, Drinks, and Gum are dangerous to computers, they ARE NOT allowed when using computers!

Handling Devices

Use two hands and walk
Horseplay is NOT allowed
Students should remain at their workstations.
Moving Around
Use two hands
Use your thumbs
Close the lid

Inappropriate Behavior

Think before you communicate using computer.
Once said, you can't ever take it back!

Content Expectations

Use educational web sites only!!
OFF LIMITS!!!!
Chat Rooms, Instant Messaging, Online Games, etc. are..
Social sites and programs need Teacher Permission!

Search Expectations

Online Research Tools with Teacher permission.

Use Safe Sites First

Ask Kids
Kid Clicks
Google Kids

Image Sites

Pics4Learning
FreeDigitalPhotos
Adjust Safe Search Settings

Password Expectations

Do not share your password.
Choose a password that you can remember!
Rude to look while someone types password
Never use someone else's login and password.

Keeping Safe on the Net

Information to students
Feel worried or upset, tell an adult.
If something comes on the screen that you don't like, just turn off the screen.
Don't communicate with people you don't know.
Keep your personal information private.
Here is what I have been discussing with students in the MS with regards to internet safety

Computer Expectations

Please leave desktop settings alone!
Conserve resources - print only when necessary.

Resource Expectations

Obey copyright laws - use proper citation when doing research.

What Happens if I Don't Follow the Expectations?

No Computer use for day
Self Evaluation & Parent Notification
Account Suspended till Meeting with Counselor, Parents, & Teacher
Report to Principal

Professional Development

It is important to offer technology related professional development in order to help instill the skills into the teachers' available skills and knowledge. This will help encourage them to take on more technology related projects in their classroom and to be more self sufficient. There are many strategies for administering professional development to staff, each with a benefit and drawback.

The main focus however should remain on big picture aspects of technology integration as opposed to small skill sets. In other words, PD should target methodologies and pedagogy related to technology integration and skills, an example would be Digital Citizenship lesson ideas as opposed to how to use MS Word.

Areas of Focus for Teacher Training

The many topics that teachers should be taught include applications, devices, curriculum integration, classroom management. The most basic of the topics include the applications and devices, often referred to as software and hardware. This takes a great deal of time to teach if a staff is not trained or has had little exposure to technology. This is the building blocks of any successful program but actually impacts student learning the least. There is always a danger of spending too much time on this area.

> *"Programs are often single-shot and mandated rather than selected by the participant, and the content often focuses on adding something new rather than improving what a teacher is already doing."* -Boss, Suzie; Jane Krauss (2009-08-03). Reinventing Project-Based Learning: Your Field Guide to Real-World Projects in the Digital Age (p. 31). International Society for Technology in Education. Kindle Edition.

Curriculum integration is by far the most important aspect of a technology integrationist job. It takes the most time and relies heavily on the participation of the teaching staff. Depending on the model and amount of involvement of the integrationist, this area of focus has varying degrees of a teacher's background knowledge as a requirement.

> *"fundamental program changes you make will require frequent and intentional collaboration with your colleagues."* -Boss, Suzie; Jane Krauss (2009-08-03). Reinventing Project-Based Learning: Your Field Guide to Real-World Projects in the Digital Age (p. 31). International Society for Technology in Education. Kindle Edition.

The final area of focus is the management of how to integrate technology into the classroom where it will have a positive impact on student learning. This aspect is often overlooked or not even brought up. However, it has the most impact on whether or not technology in the classroom will have a positive effect on student learning. If teachers are not prepared for the integration of technology in their classrooms, it may actually have a negative impact on a student's ability to learn.

Variety of PD

Having a variety of PD available for teachers is critical for a successful program. Trying to dictate one type of PD or favoring one over the other will not guarantee that all teachers get the skills they need. Time as well as experience play into the equation of different types of PD that should be offered. Forcing or only offering one type of PD will discourage teachers from attending. If participation is low, think about offering different types of PD and during different times of the day.

Many types of PD need to be offered in order to fill the needs of teachers.

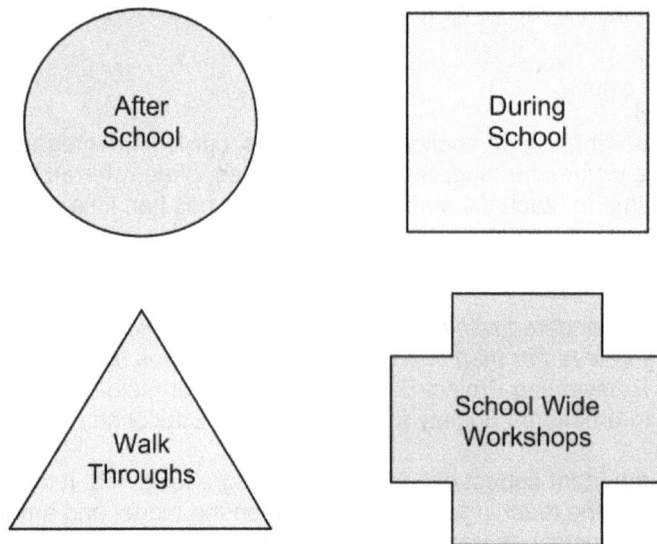

After School

During School

Walk Throughs

School Wide Workshops

PDI Versus PD

Holding just PD would be just as wrong as only teaching technology to students. The best plan of action would be to incorporate PD with student integration, otherwise known as PDI. The method for achieving this is often complex but rewarding. The first and most important aspect of PDI is to understand the needs of the school. This includes parents, students, and teachers.

Get a Pulse
Sending out and doing walk throughs is a great way to get a pulse of the needs of your school.

Core Unit Development
Once the needs are known, the integrationist who is knowledgeable in the field of technology can better determine what the focus of the year should be. Sometimes the core units will spill over into additional years. The key is to concentrate on a small number of core units as these are the main points of the PDI. Addition filler topics can be included but not made mandatory. Only the Core Units should be mandatory and these are few. This will ensure that teachers are not overburdened by technology. The Core Units can include multiple lessons to ensure that the skills are solidified by both the students and the teachers.

Grade or Subject Level Meetings
An important and critical part of PDI is collaboration with teachers. If the teachers don't buy into the program most of the effort will be lost and the participants will not gain from the experience. Using the meeting time to go over the core units and additional subjects will make sure that the PDI is tied into the curriculum and is meaningful

RSVP

Have teachers invite the integrationist into their room to teach the Core Units to both the teachers and the students at the same time. The teacher should be sending the invitation. The will give achieve a higher level of self motivation from the teacher.

The List

Have a list of teachers who have participated. Once the teacher has accomplished a goal of PDI check them off and they should be awarded a certificate including the credit hours and subjects.

Pitfalls of PD

The Dragnet

The most important part of PD or PDI is motivation. If teachers, students, and parents don't see the value of what is being taught, they won't use it. A phrase to describe ineffectual PD would be "*in one ear and out another*". Forcing or making mandatory PD will get some teachers to use what is being taught, but many others will fall through the cracks. A typical scenario would be a school offering or concentrating on only one form of PD, and not doing PDI, and "*highly encouraging*" teachers to participate. Trying to strong arm busy teachers into PD is wrong and will not be very successful. A high number may participate, which looks good for the program, but the true test is whether real learning tied to curriculum is taking place in the classroom using the tools taught.

Teachers come with many different experience and skill sets. Having a variety of options and using a more friendly approach to PD will go a long way in motivating and making everyone feel respected.

Strategy for PD

As with the multiple types of PD, there are different strategies for implementing PD whether it be application or skill. The preferred method of delivering training it to tie it in with curriculum, otherwise know as Professional Development & Integration, or PDI.

Basic Level PD Strategy

Probably the most common type of PD even at conferences is the basic level. Even integrationists that have been in the field use this strategy often.
- Single solution or topic
- Narrow focus
- No tie in to standards and benchmarks
- No alternatives given

High Level PDI Strategy

The hardest strategy to use of giving PD is to have a well rounded approach.
- Tie in to Standards and benchmarks
- Explanation of alternatives of every level
- Topic not focused on single application
- Examples of how it can be tied into core curriculum

Key Components to Well Rounded PDI Session

- **Explain the purpose or target goal of the PDI.** This step can include examples or theoretical situations.
- **Finding out about the audience** is critical especially when dealing with technology. People usually come with a wide variety of skill sets, which can make understanding difficult for some and boring for others. Having an idea of your audiences range of skills will give the presenter a guide at which to pace the presentation.
- Explain the core aspect, **benefits and drawbacks**, of the application or skill that will be discussed.
- **Show a variety of solutions** that will solve or get the group to the targeted goal. This should include demonstrating how combinations of other technology solutions in conjunction with core curriculum will make for a dynamic use of technology in the classroom.
- Close with a **tie in to standards and benchmarks**. (ISTE's NETS)
- **Example** if available.

Types of PD

There are three important places to find what should be taught in the PD workshops from the teachers and their wants and needs, from the technology integrationists and their expert perspectives, and having open sessions for all the loose ends that come up throughout the year.

Flexible PD (Best Option)

The best option for PD is to have a certificate program where teachers are required to earn one certificate per term. This keeps the burden of finding time to do the PD to a minimum, yet gives the teachers enough new skills to incorporate technology into projects. It needs to be mandatory otherwise teachers will not make time for the PD. Having the certificates awarded will keep them motivated enough to participate as well. The certificates if signed by the director should be honored by most licensure organizations for district PD requirements. Teachers can in addition earn the certificates and fulfill the technology PD requirement by scheduling training sessions during their free time during or after school. Also, they can always go to a normal scheduled PD session during or after school.

Grade Level PD

Having a grade level as a team do PD is a perfect way to make sure that all teachers doing a project have the necessary skills needed. Also, all students will get the same instruction regarding the technology skills.

Integrated PD

Integrating PD while teaching or helping with a lesson takes the most effort as each class will have to have the lesson taught to ensure full coverage. However it guarantees that all staff and students are trained. Finding a integrationist with the needed people skills is also difficult to do. If a personable integrationist is available, staff members will be more willing to have them help out in their classroom. Another benefit to integrating PD into lessons for students is that the technology integrationist is an expert and has the knowledge needed to answer questions and work around problematic issues that may arise unlike a teacher who has had limited or insufficient PD.

During School PD

Holding a PD session during a scheduled professional development day held by the school is often the best choice, since teachers are required to be there. However, try to break down PD into small sessions of no more than 10 teachers. Also, make sure all PD training is hands-on. If teachers don't get to practice what you are teaching, then it can more than likely be sent via email or posted on a ho-to web page where teachers can view and learn at their leisure.

After School PD

Holding an after school professional development session can be difficult in that many teachers use this time to catch up on their day. Also, teachers often have parents teacher meetings scheduled.

Holding an after school club for both students and teachers is another option that can be very successful for all.

2 Minute Tech Tips

Using general staff meetings is a perfect time to get a message or tech tips out to the whole staff where an email is not the best approach. Also, it helps staff get to know the Technology Coordinator on a more personal; level, which will help in building relationships.

Professional Development Tips

- Avoid syntax ladened discussion or requirements
- Avoid conformity of individual teaching styles
- Don't treat teachers with non-regard to their professionalism

Student Led

Having students leading professional development is a perfect way for students to share their expertise. In addition it gives them an opportunity to be in a leading role, thereby helping them with filling out their resumes for college.

Online Ready Made

There are a variety of ready made podcasts/screencasts/YouTube resources available online. There are many sources and levels ready to be watched. Companies, schools, and enthusiastic individuals create these videos to help others, often times they are free. They can be comprehensive, such as a course, or quick tips taking only a few minutes to everything in between. These are a perfect way to offer PD while remaining flexible and differentiating the PD itself.

Vocabulary and Legibility

All grade levels need to maintain a common vocabulary usage. This ensures that there is little confusion across the grade levels and within the scope and sequence. Lessons that introduce new words or phrases regarding technology should be noted and emphasized within the targeted lessons. They should also be reinforced before and after the target lesson and checked for understanding.

One major problem found in many classrooms is when using the Internet as a resource the reading level of material is rarely taken into consideration. Resources that use polysyllabic words and long, complex sentences are difficult for early and second language learners as well as beginning readers. This is in part due to the lack of time needed to sift through the vast amounts of resources available on the Internet. Using an online reading level tool can help teachers find appropriately leveled resources which will help students be successful. Look for online text analyzers that look for the following indicators such as Coleman Liau index, Flesh Kincaid Grade Level, ARI (Automated Readability Index), and SMOG.

Example of web site with readability tools http://www.online-utility.org/english/readability_test_and_improve.jsp

Web 2.0 & Beyond

Online applications will play a massive part in all parts of life. Work, education, and pleasure will all be affected by their use and will enhance every part of our lives. Using Web 2.0 type programs should be a part of all aspects of technology when possible to help train and create the background knowledge necessary for our students to be productive in their use.

A major concern for educators should be keeping the parents involved in every aspects of using Web 2.0 applications as they move into the parenting responsibility role. Privacy and protection of students should be paramount to the concerns of educators. Keeping the parents involved can only help keep all parties involved and feeling confident that children are being taught the right choices.

Keep parents involved and discuss the potential pitfalls of using Web 2.0 technology in the classroom whenever possible.

Digital Footprints

A major aspect of technology that must be addressed by teachers is the unknown implications of the digital footprints that we as teachers ask our students to make. Also, we must address the skills necessary to prevent unwanted or inappropriate digital footprints that students may make outside our realm of influence. Incorporating basic awareness and mini-lesson dealing with lessening the impact or making appropriate choices should be made in all lessons dealing with the Internet.

Location Aware

Another technology that will play a major role in all future aspects of teaching online applications will be location aware functions. This allows the application to note where on earth the location to be noted. As with all social media online, location aware programs use and their potential unwanted implication of use must be taken into consideration when using them in lessons or projects. Teaching students or discussing with them potential dangers or unwanted implications will help lessen any negative impacts of their use.

Year at a Glance

Starting off the year, really can start prior to the school year starting or at the tail end of the previous year.

1. Start by preparing students and parents by introducing yourself and the overarching concepts that you will be covering over the course of the school year. Send out an introductory email or newsletter is a simple way of explaining what you intend to teach. especially in a transition grade such as 5th and 8th grades.
2. Assign summer preparatory work if needed. This is a good way to insure a basic foundation of knowledge that doesn't need the guidance of the teacher.
3. Start the year off in all grades with an expectation lesson. Having parents attend or giving parents a separate skills workshop is a perfect way to build a report with parents and to set them and their children up for a successful year.
4. The beginning of the year, focus on skill building lessons that utilize the tools students will need later in the year to create well-rounded projects dealing with content from their classrooms or school-wide initiatives.
5. Mid-year have students create project utilizing multiple aspects of technology. Also, mid-year is a good time to review the expectations of technology, especially since many of them will now have a better grasp of the implications of using technology.
6. Towards the end of the year, concentrate on collaborating with the homeroom teacher. Merging the technology and the student's classroom is beneficially in many ways to everyone involved in that it produces a more real-world application of the many aspects of students learning.
7. Finally, prepare students and parents for the expectations of their next year. Wrapping-up with parents is important at the end of the year as many of them will have questions about what has been achieved over the year, and many of them will have questions and concerns about technology and their everyday

lives and interactions of their children.

Lower Elementary Lesson Ideas

The general lesson ideas are segmented by grade level. Obviously the lessons can be adapted up or down grade levels depending on the background knowledge and skills that your students population possess. There are no set dates as to when the lesson should be done. Also, ISTE's NETS are suggested and recommended.

Basic Skills - Log In/Out

Goal
Students will Apply knowledge of basic computer operations, by successfully logging in and out of computer.

Body
Talk about being a good neighbor, and how to help others. Explain mouse basics and basic keyboard layout. Demonstrate to students how to log in/out. Have them sit at a workstation and practice the skill. Vocabulary to teach: Pull-down menu, mouse, keyboard, white space. Differentiate: Use projector to demonstrate how to use the tools and to visually point out the locations on the screen. Use Google Translate for any words or phrase, which can be handed out or projected during demonstration.

Standard: Students understand human, cultural, and societal issues related to technology and practice legal and ethical behavior.
  Benchmark: exhibit a positive attitude toward using technology that supports collaboration, learning, and productivity
Standard: Students demonstrate a sound understanding of technology concepts, systems, and operations.
  Benchmark: understand and use technology systems

Basic Skills -Starting Programs

Goal
Students will Apply knowledge of basic computer operations, by successfully starting and stopping a program.

Body

Talk about being a good neighbor, and how to help others. Explain mouse basics and basic keyboard layout. Review how to log in/out. Vocabulary to teach: Dock, Pull-Down Menu, Single Click, Double Click, and Icon. Have students sit back down on carpet to demonstrate how to start/stop a program Doozla using the Dock and pull-down menu. Have them close the program and restart it. Train students using the Monitors-Off classroom management strategy. Practice it until every student can do it. Have students explore drawing a picture. Observe basic level of students. Differentiate: Use projector to demonstrate how to use the tools and to visually point out the locations on the screen. Use Google Translate for any words or phrase, which can be handed out or projected during demonstration.

Standard: Students understand human, cultural, and societal issues related to technology and practice legal and ethical behavior.
  Benchmark: exhibit a positive attitude toward using technology that supports collaboration, learning, and productivity
Standard: Students demonstrate a sound understanding of technology concepts, systems, and operations.
  Benchmark: understand and use technology systems

Basic Skills - Browser Basics

Goal
Students will Apply basic user interface techniques to navigate to specific web site.

Body

Hand out student checklist with assigned computer number. Teach students what the Internet conceptually is, and how it is made up of one big smart computer. Review with students how to start and stop the Application Safari from the Dock. Also show students how to regain the focus of an application by clicking on the Title Bar. Teach them how to enter a URL address. Have them navigate to links page. If time permits, have them find Dance Mat Typing and start the first lesson. Differentiate: Use projector to demonstrate how to use the tools and to visually point out the locations on the screen. Use Google Translate for any words or phrase, which can be handed out or projected during demonstration. Vocabulary: Dock, Title Bar, Web Address, Pull-down Menu, Return key.

Standard: Students understand human, cultural, and societal issues related to technology and practice legal and ethical behavior.
  Benchmark: exhibit a positive attitude toward using technology that supports collaboration, learning, and productivity
Standard: Students demonstrate a sound understanding of technology concepts, systems, and operations.
  Benchmark: understand and use technology systems

Basic Skills - Mouse Control

Goal

Students will Apply their knowledge of how a mouse operates and complete web based mouse lesson.

Body

Review how a Mac mouse works, and hand and finger placement, and that they can pick up the mouse. Have them navigate to Learning Links page. Demonstrate how the mouse lesson works and what is expected. When students complete a section, have them raise their hand and wait for visual check. If they finish, have them draw a picture using drawing program. Differentiate: Use projector to demonstrate how to use the tools and to visually point out the locations on the screen. Use Google Translate for any words or phrase, which can be handed out or projected during demonstration. Vocabulary: single, double, triple click; drag & drop

Standard: Students understand human, cultural, and societal issues related to technology and practice legal and ethical behavior.
  Benchmark: exhibit a positive attitude toward using technology that supports collaboration, learning, and productivity
Standard: Students demonstrate a sound understanding of technology concepts, systems, and operations.
  Benchmark: understand and use technology systems

Keyboarding 1-1

Goal

Students will Apply knowledge of keyboard layout to complete next level in the progression of the keyboarding program.

Body

Demonstrate to students how to use Tux Typing Fish Cascades to familiarize themselves with the program and the keyboard. Have students start on level EASY and do the Alphabet lesson, then the Finger Exercises. Let students know that they can return to Tux typing if they finish their daily typing lesson. Let students know that they are to use two hands while finding the letters in Tux Typing. Review with students how to navigate to online typing program. Have them complete next lesson in their self paced progression. When students finish lesson they are to raise their hand so they can be checked off. Do not let them advance, only one lesson per day. If time permits they can draw a picture using paint program. Differentiate: For students who tend to look for keys, show them how to type using the on screen finger prompts, and have them push in the keyboard drawer so they can't peek. Differentiate: Use projector to demonstrate how to use the tools and to visually point out the locations on the screen. Use Google Translate for any words or phrase, which can be handed out or projected during demonstration.

Standard: Students understand human, cultural, and societal issues related to technology and practice legal and ethical behavior.
  Benchmark: exhibit a positive attitude toward using technology that supports collaboration, learning, and productivity
Standard: Students demonstrate a sound understanding of technology concepts, systems, and operations.
  Benchmark: understand and use technology systems

Basic Skills - Browser Basics 2

Goal
Students will Apply basic user interface techniques to navigate to specific web site.

Body
Hand out student checklist with assigned computer number. Review with students what the Internet conceptually is, and how it is made up of one big smart computer. Review with students how to start and stop the Application Safari from the Dock. Also show students how to regain the focus of an application by clicking on the Title Bar. Review with them how to enter a URL address. Have them navigate to links page. If time permits, have them find Dance Mat Typing and start the first lesson. Differentiate: Use projector to demonstrate how to use the tools and to visually point out the locations on the screen. Use Google Translate for any words or phrase, which can be handed out or projected during demonstration. Vocabulary: Dock, Title Bar, Web Address, Pull-down Menu, Return key.

Standard: Students understand human, cultural, and societal issues related to technology and practice legal and ethical behavior.
  Benchmark: exhibit a positive attitude toward using technology that supports collaboration, learning, and productivity
Standard: Students demonstrate a sound understanding of technology concepts, systems, and operations.
  Benchmark: understand and use technology systems

Drawing Program Basics

Goal
Students will Create drawing of stated subject matter, by using the basic program skills demonstrated in class.

Body
Demonstrate how to use Doozla or Tux Paint drawing program. Explain the different tools and their use, explain about not restarting a picture once they start. This helps them finish on time. Explain basic format for drawings, such as name and class identifier. Once students have a foundation for the tool use, have them create a drawing using a minimum of three colors and three brushes. They should also add at least one label and or title. Students are not allowed to print unless they have been checked-off. Vocabulary: Toolbox, Home Screen Differentiate: Use projector to demonstrate how to use the tools and to visually point out the locations on the screen. Use Google Translate for any words or phrase, which can be handed out or projected during demonstration.

Standard: Students demonstrate creative thinking, construct knowledge, and develop innovative products and processes using technology
  Benchmark: create original works as a means of personal or group expression
Standard: Students understand human, cultural, and societal issues related to technology and practice legal and ethical behavior.
  Benchmark: exhibit a positive attitude toward using technology that supports collaboration, learning, and productivity
Standard: Students demonstrate a sound understanding of technology concepts, systems, and operations.
  Benchmark: understand and use technology systems

Drawing Program Print

Goal
Students will Create drawing of stated subject matter, by using the basic program skills demonstrated in class.

Body
Review how to use Doozla or Tux Paint drawing program. Explain the different tools and their use, with printing being the main focus. Explain basic format for drawings, such as name and class identifier. Once students have a foundation for the tool use, have them create a drawing using a minimum of three colors and three brushes. Also, Depending on grade level, have them write a title and-or short description of drawing. Students are not allowed to print unless they have been checked-off. Vocabulary: Toolbox, Home Screen Differentiate: Use projector to demonstrate how to use the tools and to visually point out the locations on the screen. Use Google Translate for any words or phrase, which can be handed out or projected during demonstration.

Standard: Students demonstrate creative thinking, construct knowledge, and develop innovative products and processes using technology
    Benchmark: create original works as a means of personal or group expression
Standard: Students understand human, cultural, and societal issues related to technology and practice legal and ethical behavior.
    Benchmark: exhibit a positive attitude toward using technology that supports collaboration, learning, and productivity
Standard: Students demonstrate a sound understanding of technology concepts, systems, and operations.
    Benchmark: understand and use technology systems

Keyboarding 1-2

Goal
Students will Apply knowledge of keyboard layout to complete next level in the progression of the keyboarding program.

Body
Review with students how to navigate to online typing program. Explain to them about posture and home-row. Demonstrate proper finger placement. Have them complete next lesson in their self paced progression. When students finish lesson they are to raise their hand so they can be checked off. Do not let them advance, only one lesson per day. If time permits they can draw a picture using paint program, or do Tux Typing. Differentiate: For students who tend to look for keys, show them how to type using the on screen finger prompts, have them push in the keyboard drawer so they can't peek, or use a piece of paper to cover up their hands. Differentiate: Use projector to demonstrate how to use the tools and to visually point out the locations on the screen. Use Google Translate for any words or phrase, which can be handed out or projected during demonstration. Vocabulary: Home-row, posture.

Standard: Students understand human, cultural, and societal issues related to technology and practice legal and ethical behavior.
    Benchmark: exhibit a positive attitude toward using technology that supports collaboration, learning, and productivity
Standard: Students demonstrate a sound understanding of technology concepts, systems, and operations.
    Benchmark: understand and use technology systems

Word Processor 1-1

Goal
Students will Create a word processor document, by using age appropriate document format.

Body
Explain how people use computers to write documents from email to stories. Demonstrate how to create, save, and open a digital document. Remind students about the Writing Process. Have students write what they like to eat for breakfast, then have then save document. They can use their best guess spelling. Vocabulary: Font, White Space, Word Processor, Alignment. Differentiate: For students who tend to look for keys, show them how to type using the on screen finger prompts, and have them push in the keyboard drawer so they can't peek. Differentiate: Use projector to demonstrate how to use the tools and to visually point out the locations on the screen. Use Google Translate for any words or phrase, which can be handed out or projected during

demonstration.

Standard: Students demonstrate creative thinking, construct knowledge, and develop innovative products and processes using technology
   Benchmark: create original works as a means of personal or group expression
Standard: Students understand human, cultural, and societal issues related to technology and practice legal and ethical behavior.
   Benchmark: exhibit a positive attitude toward using technology that supports collaboration, learning, and productivity
Standard: Students demonstrate a sound understanding of technology concepts, systems, and operations.
   Benchmark: understand and use technology systems

Word Processor - Formatting

Goal
Students will Create a word processor document, by using age appropriate document format.

Body
Explain how people use computers to write documents from email to stories. Review how to create, save, and open a digital document. Remind students about the Writing Process. Next demonstrate proper document formatting, such as size, font, white space, alignment, and title. Have students open previously worked on document and continue by formatting it. Then have then save document. They can use their best guess spelling until the end of writing the rough draft. Vocabulary: Font, White Space, Word Processor, Alignment. Differentiate: For students who tend to look for keys, show them how to type using the on screen finger prompts, and have them push in the keyboard drawer so they can't peek. Differentiate: Use projector to demonstrate how to use the tools and to visually point out the locations on the screen. Use Google Translate for any words or phrase, which can be handed out or projected during demonstration.

Standard: Students demonstrate creative thinking, construct knowledge, and develop innovative products and processes using technology
   Benchmark: create original works as a means of personal or group expression
Standard: Students understand human, cultural, and societal issues related to technology and practice legal and ethical behavior.
   Benchmark: exhibit a positive attitude toward using technology that supports collaboration, learning, and productivity
Standard: Students demonstrate a sound understanding of technology concepts, systems, and operations.
   Benchmark: understand and use technology systems

Voice Recording Introduction

Goal
Students will Create a voice recording, by using knowledge of software and recording techniques.

Body
Demonstrate how to use voice recording software, and how to record properly with microphone. Topics covered should be how to create a file, start and stop recording, go to beginning of recording, delete bad recording, and save recording. It is important that students understand that the room needs to be quiet in order for their classmates to record. Also, split the recording tasks with another task such as writing or drawing so not all students are recording at the same time. Have students make a test file where they say their name and what they like about school. Once recorded have them listen to their recording. If they are not pleased with it, they need to re-record. Explain the importance of accepting work that may not be perfect in order to finish task with limited time restrictions. Vocabulary: Microphone, Headset. Differentiate: For students who tend to look for keys, show them how to type using the on screen finger prompts, and have them push in the keyboard drawer so they can't peek. Differentiate: Use projector to demonstrate how to use the tools and to visually point out the locations on the screen. Use Google Translate for any words or phrase, which can be handed out or projected during

demonstration.

Standard: Students demonstrate creative thinking, construct knowledge, and develop innovative products and processes using technology
   Benchmark: create original works as a means of personal or group expression
Standard: Students understand human, cultural, and societal issues related to technology and practice legal and ethical behavior.
   Benchmark: exhibit a positive attitude toward using technology that supports collaboration, learning, and productivity
Standard: Students demonstrate a sound understanding of technology concepts, systems, and operations.
   Benchmark: understand and use technology systems

Drawing Program Save

Goal
Students will Create drawing of stated subject matter, by using the basic program skills demonstrated in class and save it.

Body
Review how to use Doozla or Tux Paint drawing program. Explain the different tools and their use, with saving being the main focus. Explain basic format for drawings, such as name and class identifier. Once students have a foundation for the tool use, have them create a drawing using a minimum of three colors and three brushes. Also, Depending on grade level, have them write a title and-or short description of drawing. Students are not allowed to print unless they have been checked-off. Vocabulary: Toolbox, Home Screen Differentiate: Use projector to demonstrate how to use the tools and to visually point out the locations on the screen. Use Google Translate for any words or phrase, which can be handed out or projected during demonstration.

Standard: Students demonstrate creative thinking, construct knowledge, and develop innovative products and processes using technology
   Benchmark: create original works as a means of personal or group expression
Standard: Students understand human, cultural, and societal issues related to technology and practice legal and ethical behavior.
   Benchmark: exhibit a positive attitude toward using technology that supports collaboration, learning, and productivity
Standard: Students demonstrate a sound understanding of technology concepts, systems, and operations.
   Benchmark: understand and use technology systems

Voice Recording - Holiday

Goal
Students will Create a voice recording, by using knowledge of software and recording techniques.

Body
Review how to use voice recording software, and how to record properly with microphone. Topics covered should be how to create a file, start and stop recording, go to beginning of recording, delete bad recording, and save recording. Review the importance that students understand that the room needs to be quiet in order for their classmates to record. Explain what background noise is. Also, split the recording tasks with another task such as writing or drawing so not all students are recording at the same time. Review what a sound wave is. Show students what a quiet and loud voice waves look like. This will help them see if they are speaking loud enough while recording. Have students make a test file where they say their name and what they like about school. Once recorded have them listen to their recording. If they are not pleased with it, they need to re-record. Explain the importance of accepting work that may not be perfect in order to finish task with limited time restrictions. Break group so every other person is recording, while the others practice typing. Once their neighbor is done recording, they can record the topic of the lesson. Vocabulary: Microphone, Headset, background noise, sound wave. Differentiate: For students who tend to look for keys, show them how to type using the on screen finger prompts, and have them push in the keyboard drawer so they can't peek. Differentiate: Use projector to demonstrate how to use the tools and to visually point out the locations on the screen. Use Google Translate for

any words or phrase, which can be handed out or projected during demonstration.

Standard: Students demonstrate creative thinking, construct knowledge, and develop innovative products and processes using technology
  Benchmark: create original works as a means of personal or group expression
Standard: Students understand human, cultural, and societal issues related to technology and practice legal and ethical behavior.
  Benchmark: exhibit a positive attitude toward using technology that supports collaboration, learning, and productivity
Standard: Students demonstrate a sound understanding of technology concepts, systems, and operations.
  Benchmark: understand and use technology systems

Voice Recording Practice

Goal
Students will Create a voice recording, by using knowledge of software and recording techniques.

Body
Review how to use voice recording software, and how to record properly with microphone. Topics covered should be how to create a file, start and stop recording, go to beginning of recording, delete bad recording, and save recording. It is important that students understand that the room needs to be quiet in order for their classmates to record. Explain what background noise is. Also, split the recording tasks with another task such as writing or drawing so not all students are recording at the same time. Explain and show what a sound wave is. Show students what a quiet and loud voice waves look like. This will help them see if they are speaking load enough while recording. Have students make a test file where they say their name and what they like about school. Once recorded have them listen to their recording. If they are not pleased with it, they need to re-record. Explain the importance of accepting work that may not be perfect in order to finish task with limited time restrictions. Vocabulary: Microphone, Headset, background noise, sound wave. Differentiate: For students who tend to look for keys, show them how to type using the on screen finger prompts, and have them push in the keyboard drawer so they can't peek. Differentiate: Use projector to demonstrate how to use the tools and to visually point out the locations on the screen. Use Google Translate for any words or phrase, which can be handed out or projected during demonstration.

Standard: Students demonstrate creative thinking, construct knowledge, and develop innovative products and processes using technology
  Benchmark: create original works as a means of personal or group expression
Standard: Students understand human, cultural, and societal issues related to technology and practice legal and ethical behavior.
  Benchmark: exhibit a positive attitude toward using technology that supports collaboration, learning, and productivity
Standard: Students demonstrate a sound understanding of technology concepts, systems, and operations.
  Benchmark: understand and use technology systems

Keyboarding 1-3

Goal
Students will Apply knowledge of keyboard layout to complete next level in the progression of the keyboarding program.

Body
Review with students how to navigate to online typing program. Explain to them about posture and home-row. Demonstrate proper finger placement using a keyboard as a prop. Demonstrate how one can angle hands so the pinkies can reach the proper key on the home-row. Also how bending the two middle fingers helps to keep fingers on home-row. Have them complete next lesson in their self paced progression. Verify that they are on the correct leveled lesson. When students

finish lesson they are to raise their hand so they can be checked off. Do not let them advance more than one lesson per day. If time permits they can draw a picture using paint program, or play Tux Typing. Students are not to disturb students who are still working on their typing lesson! Differentiate: For students who tend to look for keys, show them how to type using the on screen finger prompts, have them push in the keyboard drawer so they can't peek, or use a piece of paper to cover up their hands. Differentiate: Use projector to demonstrate how to use the tools and to visually point out the locations on the screen. Use Google Translate for any words or phrase, which can be handed out or projected during demonstration. Vocabulary: Home-row, posture.

Standard: Students understand human, cultural, and societal issues related to technology and practice legal and ethical behavior.
　Benchmark: exhibit a positive attitude toward using technology that supports collaboration, learning, and productivity
Standard: Students demonstrate a sound understanding of technology concepts, systems, and operations.
　Benchmark: understand and use technology systems

Presentation Introduction

Goal
Students will Create a presentation, by using knowledge of software and project building basics.

Body
Talk about what a presentation is and how they may have already done one, i.e. Show and Tell. Talk to them about the importance of keeping a presentation simple and not to use complete sentences. Talk to them about how added extra stuff is not necessarily a good thing and how simple is often better. Demonstrate how to use presentation software Topics covered should be how to create a file, create slides, proper formatting, and saving project. Have students make a test file where they create at least four slides, Title slide, and three Body slides. Each containing a Header and a list. Once created show students how to review their work by playing back the presentation. Explain the importance of accepting work that may not be perfect in order to finish task with limited time restrictions. Vocabulary: Slide, Title Slide, Header, Presentation, Font. Differentiate: For students who tend to look for keys, show them how to type using the on screen finger prompts, and have them push in the keyboard drawer so they can't peek. Differentiate: Use projector to demonstrate how to use the tools and to visually point out the locations on the screen. Use Google Translate for any words or phrase, which can be handed out or projected during demonstration.

Standard: Students demonstrate creative thinking, construct knowledge, and develop innovative products and processes using technology
　Benchmark: create original works as a means of personal or group expression
Standard: Students understand human, cultural, and societal issues related to technology and practice legal and ethical behavior.
　Benchmark: exhibit a positive attitude toward using technology that supports collaboration, learning, and productivity
Standard: Students demonstrate a sound understanding of technology concepts, systems, and operations.
　Benchmark: understand and use technology systems

Presentation -Move -Delete

Goal
Students will Create a presentation, by using knowledge of software and project building basics.

Body
Review how to use presentation software topics covered should be how to create a file, create slides, proper formatting, and saving project. Demonstrate how to move, and delete slides. Have students make a new test file where they create a title slide, and three additional slides. Each containing a Header and a List. Once created

show students how to review their work by playing back the presentation. Vocabulary: Header, List, Slide, Title Slide, Presentation, Font. Differentiate: For students who tend to look for keys, show them how to type using the on screen finger prompts, and have them push in the keyboard drawer so they can't peek. Differentiate: Use projector to demonstrate how to use the tools and to visually point out the locations on the screen. Use Google Translate for any words or phrase, which can be handed out or projected during demonstration.

Standard: Students demonstrate creative thinking, construct knowledge, and develop innovative products and processes using technology
Benchmark: create original works as a means of personal or group expression
Standard: Students understand human, cultural, and societal issues related to technology and practice legal and ethical behavior.
Benchmark: exhibit a positive attitude toward using technology that supports collaboration, learning, and productivity
Standard: Students demonstrate a sound understanding of technology concepts, systems, and operations.
Benchmark: understand and use technology systems

Keyboarding 1-4

Goal
Students will Apply knowledge of keyboard layout to complete next level in the progression of the keyboarding program.

Body
Review with individuals as needed how to navigate to online typing program, posture and home-row, proper finger placement, angle hands so the pinkies can reach the proper key on the home-row, how bending the two middle fingers helps to keep fingers on home-row. Have them complete next lesson in their self paced progression. Visually check that they are on the correct leveled lesson once they begin. When students finish lesson they are to raise their hand so they can be checked off. Do not let them advance more than one lesson per day. If time permits they can draw a picture using paint program, or play Tux Typing. Students are not to disturb students who are still working on their typing lesson! Differentiate: For students who tend to look for keys, show them how to type using the on screen finger prompts, have them push in the keyboard drawer so they can't peek, or use a piece of paper to cover up their hands. Differentiate: Use projector to demonstrate how to use the tools and to visually point out the locations on the screen. Use Google Translate for any words or phrase, which can be handed out or projected during demonstration. Vocabulary: Home-row, posture.

Standard: Students understand human, cultural, and societal issues related to technology and practice legal and ethical behavior.
Benchmark: exhibit a positive attitude toward using technology that supports collaboration, learning, and productivity
Standard: Students demonstrate a sound understanding of technology concepts, systems, and operations.
Benchmark: understand and use technology systems

Presentation -Images -Templates

Goal
Students will Create a presentation, by using knowledge of software and project building basics.

Body
Have them open a new presentation or one that they have been working on. Have students navigate to a web site where they can save an image on a particular topic. Have them save the image to a folder where they can get to it later. Have them Copy and Paste the URL and place it on a page in the presentation software being used. Demonstrate how to insert image. Vocabulary: Cite, Thumbnail, Template. Differentiate: For students who tend to look for keys, show them how to type using the on screen finger prompts, and have them push in the keyboard drawer so they can't peek. Differentiate: Use projector to demonstrate how to use the tools and to visually point out the locations on the screen. Use Google Translate for any words or phrase, which can be handed out or projected during demonstration.

Standard: Students demonstrate creative thinking, construct knowledge, and develop innovative products and processes using technology
  Benchmark: create original works as a means of personal or group expression
Standard: Students understand human, cultural, and societal issues related to technology and practice legal and ethical behavior.
  Benchmark: exhibit a positive attitude toward using technology that supports collaboration, learning, and productivity
Standard: Students demonstrate a sound understanding of technology concepts, systems, and operations.
  Benchmark: understand and use technology systems

Comic Life Introduction

Goal
Students will Create a digital graphic narrative, by using presentation and digital image creation software.

Body
Demonstrate how to create simple images using a simple digital painting program. Have them save a few images that can represent a story or instructions. Demonstrate how to insert images into a presentation software (Photostory for PC, Comic Life for Mac). Have them add text to their presentations. Have them save their work so they can continue another day if needed. Vocabulary: template, caption. Differentiate: For students who tend to look for keys, show them how to type using the on screen finger prompts, and have them push in the keyboard drawer so they can't peek. Differentiate: Use projector to demonstrate how to use the tools and to visually point out the locations on the screen. Use Google Translate for any words or phrase, which can be handed out or projected during demonstration.

Standard: Students demonstrate creative thinking, construct knowledge, and develop innovative products and processes using technology
  Benchmark: create original works as a means of personal or group expression
Standard: Students understand human, cultural, and societal issues related to technology and practice legal and ethical behavior.
  Benchmark: exhibit a positive attitude toward using technology that supports collaboration, learning, and productivity
Standard: Students demonstrate a sound understanding of technology concepts, systems, and operations.
  Benchmark: understand and use technology systems

Comic Life - Pictures

Goal
Students will Create a digital graphic narrative, by using presentation and digital image creation software.

Body
Demonstrate how to create simple images using a simple digital painting program. Have them 3 to 5 images that can represent a story or instructions. Have them add labels to their images. Have them save their work so they can continue another day if needed. Vocabulary: label, caption. Differentiate: For students who tend to look for keys, show them how to type using the on screen finger prompts, and have them push in the keyboard drawer so they can't peek. Differentiate: Use projector to demonstrate how to use the tools and to visually point out the locations on the screen. Use Google Translate for any words or phrase, which can be handed out or projected during demonstration.

Standard: Students demonstrate creative thinking, construct knowledge, and develop innovative products and processes using technology
  Benchmark: create original works as a means of personal or group expression
Standard: Students understand human, cultural, and societal issues related to technology and practice legal and ethical behavior.
  Benchmark: exhibit a positive attitude toward using technology that supports collaboration, learning, and productivity
Standard: Students demonstrate a sound understanding of technology concepts, systems, and operations.

Benchmark: understand and use technology systems

Comic Life - Insert Pictures

Goal

Students will Create a digital graphic narrative, by using presentation and digital image creation software.

Body

Demonstrate how to insert images into presentation software, and add text captions to help audience understand content. Have them save their work so they can continue another day if needed. Vocabulary: label, caption. Differentiate: For students who tend to look for keys, show them how to type using the on screen finger prompts, and have them push in the keyboard drawer so they can't peek. Differentiate: Use projector to demonstrate how to use the tools and to visually point out the locations on the screen. Use Google Translate for any words or phrase, which can be handed out or projected during demonstration.

Standard: Students demonstrate creative thinking, construct knowledge, and develop innovative products and processes using technology
   Benchmark: create original works as a means of personal or group expression
Standard: Students understand human, cultural, and societal issues related to technology and practice legal and ethical behavior.
   Benchmark: exhibit a positive attitude toward using technology that supports collaboration, learning, and productivity
Standard: Students demonstrate a sound understanding of technology concepts, systems, and operations.
   Benchmark: understand and use technology systems

Keyboarding 1-5

Goal

Students will Apply knowledge of keyboard layout to complete next level in the progression of the keyboarding program.

Body

Review with students how to navigate to online typing program. Explain to them about posture, keeping fingers on home-row, guessing where keys are, and only using one finger at a time. Demonstrate proper finger placement using a keyboard as a prop. Demonstrate how one can angle hands so the pinkies can reach the proper key on the home-row. Also how bending the two middle fingers helps to keep fingers on home-row. Have them complete next lesson in their self paced progression. Verify that they are on the correct leveled lesson. When students finish lesson they are to raise their hand so they can be checked off. Do not let them advance more than one lesson per day. If time permits they can draw a picture using paint program, or play Tux Typing. Students are not to disturb students who are still working on their typing lesson! Differentiate: For students who tend to look for keys, show them how to type using the on screen finger prompts, have them push in the keyboard drawer so they can't peek, or use a piece of paper to cover up their hands. Differentiate: Use projector to demonstrate how to use the tools and to visually point out the locations on the screen. Use Google Translate for any words or phrase, which can be handed out or projected during demonstration. Vocabulary: Home-row, posture.

Standard: Students understand human, cultural, and societal issues related to technology and practice legal and ethical behavior.
   Benchmark: exhibit a positive attitude toward using technology that supports collaboration, learning, and productivity
Standard: Students demonstrate a sound understanding of technology concepts, systems, and operations.
   Benchmark: understand and use technology systems

Keyboarding 1-6

Goal

Students will Apply knowledge of keyboard layout to complete next level in the progression of the keyboarding program.

Body

Remind students about posture, keeping fingers on home-row, guessing where keys are, and only using one finger at a time. Students by this point should start guessing where keys are more than looking for them. For students who are too dependent on looking, place a bent piece of paper over their hands to help instill guessing. Remind them that it will be hard at first, but it will eventually become much easier. Have them complete next lesson in their self paced progression. Verify that they are on the correct leveled lesson. When students finish lesson they are to raise their hand so they can be checked off. Do not let them advance more than one lesson per day. If time permits they can draw a picture using paint program, or play Tux Typing. Students are not to disturb students who are still working on their typing lesson! Differentiate: For students who tend to look for keys, show them how to type using the on screen finger prompts, have them push in the keyboard drawer so they can't peek, or use a piece of paper to cover up their hands. Differentiate: Use projector to demonstrate how to use the tools and to visually point out the locations on the screen. Use Google Translate for any words or phrase, which can be handed out or projected during demonstration. Vocabulary: Home-row, posture.

Standard: Students understand human, cultural, and societal issues related to technology and practice legal and ethical behavior.
   Benchmark: exhibit a positive attitude toward using technology that supports collaboration, learning, and productivity
Standard: Students demonstrate a sound understanding of technology concepts, systems, and operations.
   Benchmark: understand and use technology systems

Keyboarding 1-7

Goal

Students will Apply knowledge of keyboard layout to complete next level in the progression of the keyboarding program.

Body

Remind students about posture, keeping fingers on home-row, guessing where keys are, and only using one finger at a time. Note: Progressively challenge students to guess where the keys are. Students by this point should start guessing where keys are more than looking for them. For students who are too dependent on looking, place a bent piece of paper over their hands to help instill guessing. Remind them that it will be hard at first, but it will eventually become much easier. Have them complete next lesson in their self paced progression. Verify that they are on the correct leveled lesson. When students finish lesson they are to raise their hand so they can be checked off. Do not let them advance more than one lesson per day. If time permits they can draw a picture using paint program, or play Tux Typing. Students are not to disturb students who are still working on their typing lesson! Differentiate: For students who tend to look for keys, show them how to type using the on screen finger prompts, have them push in the keyboard drawer so they can't peek, or use a piece of paper to cover up their hands. Differentiate: Use projector to demonstrate how to use the tools and to visually point out the locations on the screen. Use Google Translate for any words or phrase, which can be handed out or projected during demonstration. Vocabulary: Home-row, posture.

Standard: Students understand human, cultural, and societal issues related to technology and practice legal and ethical behavior.
   Benchmark: exhibit a positive attitude toward using technology that supports collaboration, learning, and productivity
Standard: Students demonstrate a sound understanding of technology concepts, systems, and operations.
   Benchmark: understand and use technology systems

Word Processor -Image -Print -Spelling

Goal

Students will Create a word processor document, by using age appropriate document format.

Body

Review how to open and save, and basic formatting. Demonstrate how to use Spell Check. Have students open previously worked on document and continue revising then edit their work. Demonstrate how to insert an image into their document. Then have them print. Vocabulary: Font, White Space, Word Processor, Alignment. Differentiate: For students who tend to look for keys, show them how to type using the on screen finger prompts, and have them push in the keyboard drawer so they can't peek. Differentiate: Use projector to demonstrate how to use the tools and to visually point out the locations on the screen. Use Google Translate for any words or phrase, which can be handed out or projected during demonstration.

Standard: Students demonstrate creative thinking, construct knowledge, and develop innovative products and processes using technology
   Benchmark: create original works as a means of personal or group expression
Standard: Students understand human, cultural, and societal issues related to technology and practice legal and ethical behavior.
   Benchmark: exhibit a positive attitude toward using technology that supports collaboration, learning, and productivity
Standard: Students demonstrate a sound understanding of technology concepts, systems, and operations.
   Benchmark: understand and use technology systems

Word Processor -Title -Align -Print

Goal
Students will Create a word processor document, by using age appropriate document format.

Body
Review how to open and save, and basic formatting. Demonstrate how to use Alignment function. Have students open previously worked on document and continue revising then edit their work. Then have them print. Vocabulary: Font, White Space, Word Processor, Alignment. Differentiate: For students who tend to look for keys, show them how to type using the on screen finger prompts, and have them push in the keyboard drawer so they can't peek. Differentiate: Use projector to demonstrate how to use the tools and to visually point out the locations on the screen. Use Google Translate for any words or phrase, which can be handed out or projected during demonstration.

Standard: Students demonstrate creative thinking, construct knowledge, and develop innovative products and processes using technology
   Benchmark: create original works as a means of personal or group expression
Standard: Students understand human, cultural, and societal issues related to technology and practice legal and ethical behavior.
   Benchmark: exhibit a positive attitude toward using technology that supports collaboration, learning, and productivity
Standard: Students demonstrate a sound understanding of technology concepts, systems, and operations.
   Benchmark: understand and use technology systems

Mind Mapping -Introduction

Goal
Students will Create a visual representation of their ideas, by using mind mapping software.

Body
Explain to students what a mind map is. Show them what a hand drawn one looks like using the projector. Explain main idea, branch, and indent. Demonstrate how to make a mind map using free online program. Have them print out their mind maps. Vocabulary: Tab key, Outline, Mind Map, branch, indent, outdent. Differentiate: For students who tend to look for keys, show them how to type using the on screen finger prompts, and have them push in the keyboard drawer so they can't peek. Differentiate: Use projector to demonstrate how to use the tools and to visually point out the locations on the screen. Use Google Translate for any words or phrase, which can be handed out or projected during demonstration.

Standard: Students use critical thinking skills to plan and conduct research, manage projects, solve problems,

and make informed decisions using appropriate digital tools and resources.
Benchmark: plan and manage activities to develop a solution or complete a project
Standard: Students understand human, cultural, and societal issues related to technology and practice legal and
ethical behavior.
Benchmark: exhibit a positive attitude toward using technology that supports collaboration, learning, and
productivity
Standard: Students demonstrate a sound understanding of technology concepts, systems, and operations.
Benchmark: understand and use technology systems

Mind Mapping -Practice

Goal
Students will Create a visual representation of their ideas, by using mind mapping software.

Body
Review with students what a mind map is. Demonstrate how to make a mind map using client based Mind
Mapping software. Have them create mind map with at least three nodes, and three sub nodes, save their mind
maps. Vocabulary: Tab key, Outline, Mind Map, branch, indent, outdent. Differentiate: For students who tend to
look for keys, show them how to type using the on screen finger prompts, and have them push in the keyboard
drawer so they can't peek. Differentiate: Use projector to demonstrate how to use the tools and to visually point
out the locations on the screen. Use Google Translate for any words or phrase, which can be handed out or
projected during demonstration.

Standard: Students use critical thinking skills to plan and conduct research, manage projects, solve problems,
and make informed decisions using appropriate digital tools and resources.
Benchmark: plan and manage activities to develop a solution or complete a project
Standard: Students understand human, cultural, and societal issues related to technology and practice legal and
ethical behavior.
Benchmark: exhibit a positive attitude toward using technology that supports collaboration, learning, and
productivity
Standard: Students demonstrate a sound understanding of technology concepts, systems, and operations.
Benchmark: understand and use technology systems

Mind Mapping -Application

Goal
Students will Create a visual representation of their ideas, by using mind mapping software.

Body
Review with students about different aspects of mind mapping. Have them create mind map with at least three
nodes, and three sub nodes, save their mind maps, or have them finish/revise/edit previously
worked on mind map. Vocabulary: Node, Tab key, Outline, Mind Map, branch, indent, outdent.
Differentiate: For students who tend to look for keys, show them how to type using the on
screen finger prompts, and have them push in the keyboard drawer so they can't peek.
Differentiate: Use projector to demonstrate how to use the tools and to visually point out the
locations on the screen. Use Google Translate for any words or phrase, which can be handed
out or projected during demonstration.

Standard: Students use critical thinking skills to plan and conduct research, manage projects, solve problems,
and make informed decisions using appropriate digital tools and resources.
Benchmark: plan and manage activities to develop a solution or complete a project
Standard: Students understand human, cultural, and societal issues related to technology and practice legal and
ethical behavior.
Benchmark: exhibit a positive attitude toward using technology that supports collaboration, learning, and
productivity
Standard: Students demonstrate a sound understanding of technology concepts, systems, and operations.
Benchmark: understand and use technology systems

Go Places Safely

Goal

Communicate that computers can be used to visit far-off places and learn new things. Recall that cyberspace travel should include adult supervision.

Body

Introduce (offline) Invite children to go on an imaginary field trip. Have them pantomime the adventure as you narrate. (For example: Put on your jacket; climb on/off the bus; get your ticket punched and enter!) Teach 1 (online) Tell children another way to visit interesting places around the world is through the computer. Take students to Cybersmart, click on Student Links, and then click on the CIRCLE. Find the title of this lesson, and open its links. Choose a site to explore with the class. Allow the children to decide where to go in the site and in what order. Guide them in making choices and read aloud any relevant text. Teach 2 (offline) Distribute Activity Sheet 1. Invite students to imagine some exciting places to visit in cyberspace. Children can draw their own pictures. Teach 3 (offline) Tell children to always take a grown-up when they go places on the computer, just as they do when going to the zoo or any other place. If time permits Distribute Activity Sheet 2 for children to color as they discuss the rule they just learned. Close (offline) Ask: How is using the computer to visit a place different from really going to the place? Discuss the ease and speed of traveling via the computer. Ask: What same rule do we have for visiting a new place using a computer or in real life? Direct the discussion to the need to travel with an adult whether online or on a real trip. Extend (offline) The following activity can be added for students who completed this lesson in a previous grade. Ask children to make a collage depicting the kinds of information that should be kept private. They can print their names and draw pictures or cut magazine photos to represent their homes. Explain that, just as they do not tell their name or address to strangers, they should not type such private information into the computer without the permission of their teacher or parent.

Standard: Students apply digital tools to gather, evaluate, and use information.
   Benchmark: plan strategies to guide inquiry
Standard: Students apply digital tools to gather, evaluate, and use information.
   Benchmark: locate, organize, analyze, evaluate, synthesize, and ethically use information from a variety of
           sources and media
Standard: Students understand human, cultural, and societal issues related to technology and practice legal and
           ethical behavior.
   Benchmark: advocate and practice safe, legal, and responsible use of information and technology
Standard: Students understand human, cultural, and societal issues related to technology and practice legal and
           ethical behavior.
   Benchmark: exhibit a positive attitude toward using technology that supports collaboration, learning, and
           productivity
Standard: Students demonstrate a sound understanding of technology concepts, systems, and operations.
   Benchmark: understand and use technology systems

Is This Yours?

Goal

Recognize that objects, including computer equipment, have owners -Identify the school as the owner of its computers and related equipment -Demonstrate respect for the property of other people and the school

Body

Before class, have five children each remove one shoe. Place the shoes in a large bag or box. Have children sit in a circle. Reach into the bag and pull out one shoe. Ask: Whose shoe is this? Allow children to guess before the owner raises his or her hand. -As you return each shoe, ask: Does this shoe belong to you? (Yes, that shoe belongs to me.) Have children put their shoes back on. Teach 1 -Walk around the room, pointing to objects (for example: backpacks, lunch boxes, items on the teacher's desk, furniture, toys, and computer equipment). Have children identify each object and its owner. -Explain that everyone must show respect for the belongings of others, including things that belong to the school. Discuss ways to show respect, including asking permission to use them and being gentle when handling them. Teach 2 -Distribute the activity sheet. -Discuss the situation pictured. Have children guess the objects to which the boy is referring (desk, chair, computer, backpack, scarf, toy, book, ball, or crayon). For each object, have children suggest the girl's reply. -Read the text to the children and invite them to give examples of how they wish people to respect the things they own and how they respect those that others own. Close -Ask: Name some things that belong to people. -Ask: Whose computer is that (point to one in the room)? -Ask: How do you show respect for things that belong to other people? Extend The following activity can be added for students who completed this lesson in a previous grade. -Make a "Respect Tree" from colored paper and hang it on a wall. Have children cut out green leaves and allow them to add a leaf to the tree each time one of them shows respect for the school's computers.

Standard: Students understand human, cultural, and societal issues related to technology and practice legal and ethical behavior.
   Benchmark: advocate and practice safe, legal, and responsible use of information and technology
Standard: Students understand human, cultural, and societal issues related to technology and practice legal and ethical behavior.
   Benchmark: exhibit a positive attitude toward using technology that supports collaboration, learning, and productivity

A-B-C Searching
Goal
Find the link for a specified letter of the alphabet on a children's Web site -Explain how to search online for animal pictures by using the alphabet

Body
Research and Information Fluency Introduce (offline) -Show children a picture dictionary. Explain that pictures of things that begin with A are first, followed by pictures of things that begin with B, and so on. -Ask: Where in this book will you find words that begin with Z? (On the last page.) -Tell children that they can also use letters to find pictures online. Teach 1 (online) -Take students to www.becybersmart.org or www.cybersmartcurriculum.org, click on Student Links, and then click on the circle. Find the title of this lesson, and open its links. -Have children find the alphabet display across the top of the page called "Animal Printouts." -Click on the letter A to find pictures of animals whose names begin with that letter. -Demonstrate how to scroll along the A page, allowing the class to choose an animal and click on its name or picture. -Print two copies of the page for the selected animal. Teach 2 (online) -Allow each child to click on a letter, choose an animal, click its link, and print two copies. -Ask children to color the pictures on their two animal printouts. Teach 3 (offline) -Distribute the activity sheet. -Have children color the alphabet and then write the letter they used to search online. -Help them staple one copy of their animal printout to the activity sheet. Close (offline) -Collect the remaining animal printout from each child. As they hand them to you, ask: What letter did you use to search for animals? Assemble an "Animal Alphabet" display or booklet by posting or binding the animal printouts in order, each labeled with the letter of the alphabet used to find it. Extend (offline) The following activity can be added for students who completed this lesson in a previous grade. -Have children suggest the names of animals, identify their first letter, and search for that animal in the "Animal Printouts" site. Differentiate: For students who tend to look for keys, show them how to type using the on screen finger prompts, and have them push in the keyboard drawer so they can't peek. Differentiate: Use projector to demonstrate how to use the tools and to visually point out the locations on the screen. Use Google Translate for any words or phrase, which can be handed out or projected during demonstration.

Standard: Students apply digital tools to gather, evaluate, and use information.
   Benchmark: plan strategies to guide inquiry
Standard: Students apply digital tools to gather, evaluate, and use information.
   Benchmark: locate, organize, analyze, evaluate, synthesize, and ethically use information from a variety of sources and media

Good Sites
Goal
Rate features of an informational site. Explain that not everyone will rate a site the same way

Body
Introduce (offline) -Have children identify something about their school with which they are all familiar - for

example, the color of walls in the school cafeteria. -Ask: Do you like the color of the walls? Have children who wish to answer "yes" raise their hands. Then have children answering "no" raise their hands. -Point out that people can have different ideas about what colors, stories, movies - or even Web sites - they like. Teach 1 (online) -Take children to www.becybersmart.org or www.cybersmartcurriculum.org, click on Student Links, and then click on the circle. -Explore one of the sites with the class, inviting children to tell what they like and do not like about it. Teach 2 (online) -Distribute the activity sheet, telling children they will use it to record what they like and do not like about the Web site. -Explain that for each question, children should trace and color the happy face if their answer is "yes" and the sad face if their answer is "no." -For "Do you like the words?" tell children to think about how well they can understand the text when it is read aloud. -Follow the same procedure with the remaining four criteria. Help children consider whether the pictures are helpful and provide new information, if the colors and patterns are pleasing or jarring and distracting, how many links work or lead to dead ends, and whether they would recommend the site to friends. Teach 3 (online) -When children have finished rating the site, ask: How many happy faces did you give this site in all? -Explain that children may have different ideas about the Web site and this is why children's totals will vary. -Download the home page of the site and make a copy for each child to staple to his or her activity sheet. Close (offline) -Ask: What does it mean if you give a Web site all happy faces? (It means the Web site is very good.) -Ask: Will all children answer the questions in the same way? Why or why not? (Probably not, because not everyone likes the same things.) Extend (online) The following activity can be added for students who completed this lesson in a previous grade. -Ask: Do you think you will like some Web sites better than others? Have children explore and evaluate two other sites selected for this lesson, using a copy of the activity sheet to record their responses. Then have them compare the total number of happy faces they awarded each site and conclude which site they liked best. -Have students review the Activity Sheet and ask: What other words might describe a good site? Allow students to dictate additional questions to answer when evaluating Web sites.

Standard: Students apply digital tools to gather, evaluate, and use information.
   Benchmark: locate, organize, analyze, evaluate, synthesize, and ethically use information from a variety of
           sources and media

The Library

Goal
Identify several activities offered at the library. Explain that the librarian can help find information in the library

Body
Introduce -Ask: Have you ever visited a library? What did you do there? -Tell children that today they will pretend they are at the library and learn some things to do there. Teach 1 -Distribute Activity Sheet 1. -Tell children that the picture shows a library and have them describe everything they see. -Ask: What seems to be missing from this picture? Encourage children to predict what kinds of pictures will fill in the blank spaces. Teach 2 -Distribute Activity Sheet 2. -Have children cut out, match, and paste each rectangle to the corresponding rectangle on Activity Sheet 1. They can then color their completed activity sheet. -Discuss the activities represented by the items in the rectangles as children assemble their sheets, pointing out all the resources and different media available at the library besides books. (listen to tapes, watch videos, use the computer, go into cyberspace) -Have children imagine that they want to learn about the moon. Ask: Who in the library can help you find what you want? Discuss how the librarian's job is to help them find the information they need. Close - Ask: What can you do at the library? -Ask: What is the librarian's job? (to help children find books and tapes, to show them how to use the computer, and to take them online) Extend The following activity can be added for students who completed this lesson in a previous grade. -Review the contents of the lesson and then take children to their school or community library. Ask the librarian to help them explore a favorite Web site. Differentiate: For students who tend to look for keys, show them how to type using the on screen finger prompts, and have them push in the keyboard drawer so they can't peek. Differentiate: Use projector to demonstrate how to use the tools and to visually point out the locations on the screen. Use Google Translate for any words or phrase, which can be handed out or projected during demonstration.

Standard: Students understand human, cultural, and societal issues related to technology and practice legal and
           ethical behavior.
   Benchmark: exhibit a positive attitude toward using technology that supports collaboration, learning, and
           productivity

Standard: Students understand human, cultural, and societal issues related to technology and practice legal and ethical behavior.

Benchmark: exhibit leadership for digital citizenship

Keyboarding 1-8

Goal

Students will Apply knowledge of keyboard layout to complete next level in the progression of the keyboarding program.

Body

Remind students about posture, keeping fingers on home-row, guessing where keys are, and only using one finger at a time. Note: Progressively challenge students to guess where the keys are. Students by this point should start guessing where keys are more than looking for them. For students who are too dependent on looking, place a bent piece of paper over their hands to help instill guessing. Remind them that it will be hard at first, but it will eventually become much easier. Have them complete next lesson in their self paced progression. Verify that they are on the correct leveled lesson. When students finish lesson they are to raise their hand so they can be checked off. Do not let them advance more than one lesson per day. If time permits they can draw a picture using paint program, or play Tux Typing. Students are not to disturb students who are still working on their typing lesson! Differentiate: For students who tend to look for keys, show them how to type using the on screen finger prompts, have them push in the keyboard drawer so they can't peek, or use a piece of paper to cover up their hands. Differentiate: Use projector to demonstrate how to use the tools and to visually point out the locations on the screen. Use Google Translate for any words or phrase, which can be handed out or projected during demonstration. Vocabulary: Home-row, posture.

Standard: Students understand human, cultural, and societal issues related to technology and practice legal and ethical behavior.

Benchmark: exhibit a positive attitude toward using technology that supports collaboration, learning, and productivity

Standard: Students demonstrate a sound understanding of technology concepts, systems, and operations.

Benchmark: understand and use technology systems

Find the Ad

Goal

Objectives -Identify ads as links to sites trying to sell something -Distinguish ads from content at children's sites

Body

Introduce (offline) -Ask: What is the purpose of a television commercial? Help children understand that television commercials are intended to make people want to buy something. -Explain that another word for commercial is "ad" and that in this lesson they will look for ads in cyberspace. Teach 1 (online) -Take students to www.becybersmart.org or www.cybersmartcurriculum.org, click on Student Links, and then click on the circle. Find the title of this lesson, and open its links. Choose a site to explore with the class. -Ask: What can children do at this site? Help them describe the activities offered and discuss the content of the site. Teach 2 (online) - Once children have explored the content, point out an ad. Discuss how to distinguish the ads at a children's site. NOTE: In most cases, the ads are labeled "AD." Banner ads (horizontal rectangles) are usually at the top of a page; button ads (small squares) and ads of other shapes and sizes may be placed along the sides and bottom. -Ask: What do you think this ad is trying to do? (Encourage people to buy something.) -Ask: What happens if you click on the ad? Demonstrate how clicking on an ad takes them away from what they were doing. Explain that the ad is there to sell something to children or their parents. -Show children how to use the Back button to return to the site they were enjoying. Teach 3 (offline) -Distribute the activity sheet. -Tell children to pretend they are looking at a Web page. Ask: What is this page about? (It is a story of the Three Little Pigs.) -Have children locate the ad. Ask: What is pretty or fun about the ad? (The ad has a clown that wants to have fun.) -Allow children to color the picture, suggesting that they use different colors for the ad and the story. Close (offline) - Ask: What is the purpose of an ad? (to get you to buy something) -Ask: How can you find an ad at a children's site? (look at the top, bottom, or sides of the page for a rectangle, or box, with the word "AD") Extend (offline) The following activity can be added for students who completed this lesson in a previous grade. -Have children explore advertising across several media. Allow them to create displays representing advertisements in magazines, newspapers, on television, and on Web sites. Differentiate: For students who tend to look for keys, show them how to type using the on screen finger prompts, and have them push in the keyboard drawer so they can't peek. Differentiate: Use projector to demonstrate how to use the tools and to visually point out the locations on the screen. Use Google Translate for any words or phrase, which can be handed out or projected during demonstration.

Standard: Students apply digital tools to gather, evaluate, and use information.
  Benchmark: locate, organize, analyze, evaluate, synthesize, and ethically use information from a variety of sources and media

Spread the News!

Goal
Overview Children learn what it means to communicate, recognize the computer as a communication invention, and plan their own way to communicate a message. Objectives -Define "communicate" -Describe communications inventions -Recognize the computer as a device used to communicate Students will Remember|Understand|Apply|Analyze|Evaluate|

Body
Introduce -Pose the following to children: Our school's principal has some very exciting news to tell. How will he communicate the news to children? To teachers? To parents? To the neighborhood? List children's ideas about which communications methods to use, encouraging them to consider the best method for each audience. Teach 1 -Have children reflect on the story about the principal's news and tell what the word "communicate" means. Summarize responses that reflect the conveying of information (for example: to tell, to announce, to speak, to write). -Ask: How do we communicate in our classroom? (by speaking; by writing; by drawing; by raising our hands; by smiling or other facial expressions) Teach 2 -Have children plan a way to communicate something exciting to the whole school. (Children might enjoy creating a "pretend" event such as a horse visiting the school.) Tell children they must communicate the news without speaking, but can use their faces, hands, other parts of their body, or special tools. -As a class, plan how they will communicate their message. Have them consider how they will deliver their message around the school. Teach 3 -Distribute the activity sheet. -For each picture, ask: What is this invention called? How is it used to communicate? Many children think of the computer as primarily a device for playing games. Encourage them to think of it as a communication device, like a telephone. -Invite children to color the picture of the child using the computer. As they do, explain that computers can be used to send messages from one person to another. Invite children to share their knowledge of E-mail. Assess The following items assess student mastery of the lesson objectives. -Ask: What does "communicate" mean? -Ask: What kinds of inventions are used to communicate? -Ask: How is a computer used to communicate? Extend The following activity can be added for students who completed this lesson in a previous grade. -Have children draw or cut out pictures and use them to make a collage showing a variety of inventions used to communicate (for example, telephones, computers, cell phones, beepers, letters, radios, televisions, and posters). Differentiate: For students who tend to look for keys, show them how to type using the on screen finger prompts, and have them push in the keyboard drawer so they can't peek. Differentiate: Use projector to demonstrate how to use the tools and to visually point out the locations on the screen. Use Google Translate for any words or phrase, which can be handed out or projected during demonstration.

Standard: Students demonstrate a sound understanding of technology concepts, systems, and operations.
  Benchmark: transfer current knowledge to learning of new technologies
Standard: Students demonstrate a sound understanding of technology concepts, systems, and operations.
  Benchmark: understand and use technology systems

Cyberspace at School

Goal
Overview Children explore the concept of cyberspace as a means of communicating with real people within their school. -Explain that cyberspace is a means of communicating with real people -Draw pictures to show cyberspace connections between real people

Body

Introduce -Have children list all the ways they can send and receive messages (write, draw, telephone, fax, mail, etc.) Teach 1 -Present the following to children: I'd like to tell Ms. (a teacher in a distant classroom) some important news. I can't go and tell her now, because I am teaching in this room. Ask: How will I get the message to her? Students may suggest using an intercom or sending a student with a written note. -Explain that there is another way to deliver the news without anyone needing to leave the room - by sending the message through cyberspace using the computer. -Invite children to watch you type a brief E-mail message, fill in the header information, and click the button to send it. OPTIONAL: Alert the recipient to watch for the E-mail and to reply as soon as it is received. -Ask: Where did my message go? How did it happen? Guide children to use the word "cyberspace" in their responses. Teach 2 -Ask: How could you send a message to another teacher in our school? To our principal? To the nurse? Guide children to recognize that messages can be sent through cyberspace to reach all of these people. -Distribute the activity sheet. Have children think of the message you sent to another teacher and all the other real people they might send a message to through cyberspace and then draw a picture of the cyberspace connections between them. Encourage them to think imaginatively and show how people communicate by using computers. Teach 3 - Invite volunteers to share their drawings and to explain how people in their school communicate through cyberspace. While there is no right or wrong way to draw cyberspace, children's pictures should show their understanding that cyberspace is a way for real people to communicate by using computers. Assess The following items assess student mastery of the lesson objectives. -Ask: What can you do in cyberspace? (send messages to real people) - Ask: What did your pictures show? Extend The following activity can be added for students who completed this lesson in a previous grade. -Help children make a list of people beyond their school with whom they might communicate through cyberspace (for example, a friend in another town or an uncle very far away). Then have them draw the cyberspace connections between all these people, introducing the idea that cyberspace extends beyond their school to people using computers anywhere in the world. Differentiate: For students who tend to look for keys, show them how to type using the on screen finger prompts, and have them push in the keyboard drawer so they can't peek. Differentiate: Use projector to demonstrate how to use the tools and to visually point out the locations on the screen. Use Google Translate for any words or phrase, which can be handed out or projected during demonstration.

Standard: Students demonstrate a sound understanding of technology concepts, systems, and operations.
   Benchmark: understand and use technology systems

Mind Mapping -CyberSMART

Goal

Students will Create a visual representation of their ideas, by using mind mapping software.

Body

Review with students about different aspects of mind mapping. Have them create mind map with at least three nodes, and three sub nodes, save their mind maps, or have them finish/revise/edit previously worked on mind map. Review Citation. Allow students to share ideas, but teach them to write the name of the person they got the idea from after listing the fact in a node. This will instill proper citation behavior. Vocabulary: Node, Tab key, Outline, Mind Map, branch, indent, outdent. Differentiate: For students who tend to look for keys, show them how to type using the on screen finger prompts, and have them push in the keyboard drawer so they can't peek. Differentiate: Use projector to demonstrate how to use the tools and to visually point out the locations on the screen. Use Google Translate for any words or phrase, which can be handed out or projected during demonstration.

Standard: Students use critical thinking skills to plan and conduct research, manage projects, solve problems, and make informed decisions using appropriate digital tools and resources.
   Benchmark: plan and manage activities to develop a solution or complete a project
Standard: Students understand human, cultural, and societal issues related to technology and practice legal and ethical behavior.

Benchmark: exhibit a positive attitude toward using technology that supports collaboration, learning, and productivity
Standard: Students demonstrate a sound understanding of technology concepts, systems, and operations.
    Benchmark: understand and use technology systems

Word Processor -CyberSMART

Goal
Students will Create a word processor document, by using age appropriate document format.

Body
Review how to open and save, insert image, and basic formatting. Have students import mind map outline. Have students revise work by reading aloud before printing. Vocabulary: Font, White Space, Word Processor, Alignment. Differentiate: For students who tend to look for keys, show them how to type using the on screen finger prompts, and have them push in the keyboard drawer so they can't peek. Differentiate: Use projector to demonstrate how to use the tools and to visually point out the locations on the screen. Use Google Translate for any words or phrase, which can be handed out or projected during demonstration.

Standard: Students demonstrate creative thinking, construct knowledge, and develop innovative products and processes using technology
    Benchmark: create original works as a means of personal or group expression
Standard: Students understand human, cultural, and societal issues related to technology and practice legal and ethical behavior.
    Benchmark: exhibit a positive attitude toward using technology that supports collaboration, learning, and productivity
Standard: Students demonstrate a sound understanding of technology concepts, systems, and operations.
    Benchmark: understand and use technology systems

Drawing Program -CyberSMART

Goal
Students will Create drawing of stated subject matter, by using the basic program skills demonstrated in class, save and print it.

Body
Review how to use drawing program. Review the different tools and their use. Explain basic format for drawings, such as name and class identifier. Once students have a foundation for the tool use, have them create a drawing using a minimum of three colors and three brushes. Also, Depending on grade level, have them write a title and-or short description of drawing. Students are not allowed to print unless they have been checked-off. Vocabulary: Toolbox, Home Screen Differentiate: Use projector to demonstrate how to use the tools and to visually point out the locations on the screen. Use Google Translate for any words or phrase, which can be handed out or projected during demonstration.

Standard: Students demonstrate creative thinking, construct knowledge, and develop innovative products and processes using technology
    Benchmark: create original works as a means of personal or group expression
Standard: Students understand human, cultural, and societal issues related to technology and practice legal and ethical behavior.
    Benchmark: exhibit a positive attitude toward using technology that supports collaboration, learning, and productivity
Standard: Students demonstrate a sound understanding of technology concepts, systems, and operations.
    Benchmark: understand and use technology systems

Comic Life - CyberSMART

Goal
Students will Create a digital graphic narrative, by using presentation and digital image creation software.

Body

Review how to insert images into presentation software, and add text captions to help audience understand content. Have them save their work so they can continue another day if needed. Vocabulary: label, caption. Differentiate: For students who tend to look for keys, show them how to type using the on screen finger prompts, and have them push in the keyboard drawer so they can't peek. Differentiate: Use projector to demonstrate how to use the tools and to visually point out the locations on the screen. Use Google Translate for any words or phrase, which can be handed out or projected during demonstration.

Standard: Students demonstrate creative thinking, construct knowledge, and develop innovative products and processes using technology
  Benchmark: create original works as a means of personal or group expression
Standard: Students understand human, cultural, and societal issues related to technology and practice legal and ethical behavior.
  Benchmark: exhibit a positive attitude toward using technology that supports collaboration, learning, and productivity
Standard: Students demonstrate a sound understanding of technology concepts, systems, and operations.
  Benchmark: understand and use technology systems

Online Presence Introduction

Goal

Recognize Web forms requesting private information -Recall never to submit private information to a site—even one with a favorite character—without a parent's permission

Body

Discuss with students the importance of not giving out personal information when online. Have them use online educations math site http://www.arcademicskillbuilders.com/ which is an ad free, free, and account-less web site. Vocabulary: Form Differentiate: For students who tend to look for keys, show them how to type using the on screen finger prompts, and have them push in the keyboard drawer so they can't peek. Differentiate: Use projector to demonstrate how to use the tools and to visually point out the locations on the screen. Use Google Translate for any words or phrase, which can be handed out or projected during demonstration.

Standard: Students understand human, cultural, and societal issues related to technology and practice legal and ethical behavior.
  Benchmark: advocate and practice safe, legal, and responsible use of information and technology
Standard: Students understand human, cultural, and societal issues related to technology and practice legal and ethical behavior.
  Benchmark: exhibit leadership for digital citizenship

Online Presence Nickname

Goal

Recognize Web forms requesting private information -Recall never to submit private information to a site—even one with a favorite character—without a parent's permission

Body

Review with students the importance of not giving out personal information when online. Have them use a paint program to draw a picture of a nickname they want. Have them include the written name i the drawing. Discuss with students how they are never allowed to call a person by their nickname. Have them use online educations math site http://www.arcademicskillbuilders.com/ which is an ad free, free, and account-less web site using their new nickname. Vocabulary: Form Differentiate: For students who tend to look for keys, show them how to type using the on screen finger prompts, and have them push in the keyboard drawer so they can't peek. Differentiate: Use projector to demonstrate how to use the tools and to visually point out the locations on the screen. Use Google Translate for any words or phrase, which can be handed out or projected during demonstration.

Standard: Students understand human, cultural, and societal issues related to technology and practice legal and
ethical behavior.
Benchmark: advocate and practice safe, legal, and responsible use of information and technology
Standard: Students understand human, cultural, and societal issues related to technology and practice legal and
ethical behavior.
Benchmark: exhibit leadership for digital citizenship

Google Earth Introduction

Goal
Students will apply user interface skills used, by exploring that basic usage of Google Earth.

Body
Demonstrate the use of Google Earth's basic features. Demonstrate how to use on map tools, and search box.
Once demonstrated, have students find basic geographic elements listed on checklist. Vocabulary: Collapse,
Search, Zoom-in, Zoom-out, Orient Differentiate: For students who tend to look for keys, show them how to type
using the on screen finger prompts, and have them push in the keyboard drawer so they can't peek.
Differentiate: Use projector to demonstrate how to use the tools and to visually point out the locations on the
screen. Use Google Translate for any words or phrase, which can be handed out or projected during
demonstration.

Standard: Students apply digital tools to gather, evaluate, and use information.
Benchmark: evaluate and select information sources and digital tools based on the appropriateness to specific
tasks
Standard: Students use critical thinking skills to plan and conduct research, manage projects, solve problems,
and make informed decisions using appropriate digital tools and resources.
Benchmark: collect and analyze data to identify solutions and/or make informed decisions
Standard: Students demonstrate a sound understanding of technology concepts, systems, and operations.
Benchmark: understand and use technology systems

Graphing Introduction

Goal
Students will Understand a simple bar graph, by indirectly creating a bar graph using interactive graphing
program and by completing a tutorial online.

Body
Have students or walk them through an online interactive bar graph tutorial. Afterwards have them play an
interactive online bar graph game. Observe them and ask them simple questions about their bar graphs as they
are playing to garner understanding. Vocabulary: Differentiate: For students who tend to look for keys, show
them how to type using the on screen finger prompts, and have them push in the keyboard drawer so they can't
peek. Differentiate: Use projector to demonstrate how to use the tools and to visually point out the locations on
the screen. Use Google Translate for any words or phrase, which can be handed out or projected during
demonstration.

Standard: Students demonstrate creative thinking, construct knowledge, and develop innovative products and
processes using technology
Benchmark: identify trends and forecast possibilities
Standard: Students understand human, cultural, and societal issues related to technology and practice legal and
ethical behavior.
Benchmark: demonstrate personal responsibility for lifelong learning
Standard: Students demonstrate a sound understanding of technology concepts, systems, and operations.
Benchmark: understand and use technology systems

Graphing Creation

Goal
Students will Understand a simple bar graph, by indirectly creating a bar graph using interactive graphing

program and by completing a tutorial online.

Body
Review parts of a bar graph. Have students create a simple bar graph using pre-existing data collected from another class or project. If no data is available, have them make a simple survey to ask fellow students. Only allow a short amount of time to collect data to manage time. Next explain a pictograph. Have students create another graph by surveying fellow students and graphing the data. Vocabulary: Differentiate: For students who tend to look for keys, show them how to type using the on screen finger prompts, and have them push in the keyboard drawer so they can't peek. Differentiate: Use projector to demonstrate how to use the tools and to visually point out the locations on the screen. Use Google Translate for any words or phrase, which can be handed out or projected during demonstration.

Standard: Students demonstrate creative thinking, construct knowledge, and develop innovative products and processes using technology
    Benchmark: identify trends and forecast possibilities
Standard: Students understand human, cultural, and societal issues related to technology and practice legal and ethical behavior.
    Benchmark: demonstrate personal responsibility for lifelong learning
Standard: Students demonstrate a sound understanding of technology concepts, systems, and operations.
    Benchmark: understand and use technology systems

Basic Research Introduction

Goal
Students will Understand and apply basic research fundamentals, by using research strategies pertaining to keywords and key phrases.

Body
Explain and demonstrate how to use kid friendly search engine or directory using keyword and keyphrase. Have students try using the fundamentals taught by completing a very simple worksheet. Have them try out a few different search engines/directories using simple search words and phrases. Once they are done with worksheet, have them try their new search skills to find an educational game to play. NOTE: Close supervision will be needed during this lesson. Vocabulary: Differentiate: For students who tend to look for keys, show them how to type using the on screen finger prompts, and have them push in the keyboard drawer so they can't peek. Differentiate: Use projector to demonstrate how to use the tools and to visually point out the locations on the screen. Use Google Translate for any words or phrase, which can be handed out or projected during demonstration.

Standard: Students apply digital tools to gather, evaluate, and use information.
    Benchmark: evaluate and select information sources and digital tools based on the appropriateness to specific tasks
Standard: Students understand human, cultural, and societal issues related to technology and practice legal and ethical behavior.
    Benchmark: exhibit a positive attitude toward using technology that supports collaboration, learning, and productivity
Standard: Students demonstrate a sound understanding of technology concepts, systems, and operations.
    Benchmark: understand and use technology systems

Graphing Creation 2

Goal
Students will Understand a simple bar graph, by indirectly creating a bar graph using interactive graphing program and by completing a tutorial online.

Body
Review parts of a bar graph. Have students create a simple bar graph using pre-existing data collected from another class or project. If no data is available, have them make a simple survey to ask fellow students. Only

allow a short amount of time to collect data to manage time. Next explain a pictograph. Have students create another graph by surveying fellow students and graphing the data. Vocabulary: Differentiate: For students who tend to look for keys, show them how to type using the on screen finger prompts, and have them push in the keyboard drawer so they can't peek. Differentiate: Use projector to demonstrate how to use the tools and to visually point out the locations on the screen. Use Google Translate for any words or phrase, which can be handed out or projected during demonstration.

Standard: Students demonstrate creative thinking, construct knowledge, and develop innovative products and processes using technology
   Benchmark: identify trends and forecast possibilities
Standard: Students understand human, cultural, and societal issues related to technology and practice legal and ethical behavior.
   Benchmark: demonstrate personal responsibility for lifelong learning
Standard: Students demonstrate a sound understanding of technology concepts, systems, and operations.
   Benchmark: understand and use technology systems

Summative Keyboarding
Goal
Students will demonstrate Applied knowledge of finger placement and proper keyboarding posture by completing leveled keyboarding lessons.

Body
Have students complete series of keyboarding lessons. Vocabulary: Home Row Differentiate: For students who tend to look for keys, show them how to type using the on screen finger prompts, and have them push in the keyboard drawer so they can't peek. Differentiate: Use projector to demonstrate how to use the tools and to visually point out the locations on the screen. Use Google Translate for any words or phrase, which can be handed out or projected during demonstration.
Standard: Students demonstrate a sound understanding of technology concepts, systems, and operations.
   Benchmark: understand and use technology systems

Google Earth 2
Goal
Students will apply user interface skills used, by exploring that basic usage of Google Earth.

Body
Demonstrate the use of Google Earth's basic features. Demonstrate how to collapse tool box areas. Once demonstrated, have students find basic geographic elements listed on checklist. Vocabulary: Collapse, Search, Zoom-in, Zoom-out, Orient Differentiate: For students who tend to look for keys, show them how to type using the on screen finger prompts, and have them push in the keyboard drawer so they can't peek. Differentiate: Use projector to demonstrate how to use the tools and to visually point out the locations on the screen. Use Google Translate for any words or phrase, which can be handed out or projected during demonstration.

Standard: Students apply digital tools to gather, evaluate, and use information.
   Benchmark: evaluate and select information sources and digital tools based on the appropriateness to specific tasks
Standard: Students use critical thinking skills to plan and conduct research, manage projects, solve problems, and make informed decisions using appropriate digital tools and resources.
   Benchmark: collect and analyze data to identify solutions and/or make informed decisions
Standard: Students understand human, cultural, and societal issues related to technology and practice legal and ethical behavior.
   Benchmark: exhibit a positive attitude toward using technology that supports collaboration, learning, and productivity
Standard: Students demonstrate a sound understanding of technology concepts, systems, and operations.
   Benchmark: understand and use technology systems

Google Earth 3

Goal

Students will apply user interface skills used, by exploring that basic usage of Google Earth.

Body

Demonstrate the use of Google Earth's basic features. Demonstrate how to use search box and to look at results, then choose the best guess from selection. Once demonstrated, have students find basic geographic elements listed on checklist. Vocabulary: Collapse, Search, Zoom-in, Zoom-out, Orient Differentiate: For students who tend to look for keys, show them how to type using the on screen finger prompts, and have them push in the keyboard drawer so they can't peek. Differentiate: Use projector to demonstrate how to use the tools and to visually point out the locations on the screen. Use Google Translate for any words or phrase, which can be handed out or projected during demonstration.

Standard: Students apply digital tools to gather, evaluate, and use information.
  Benchmark: evaluate and select information sources and digital tools based on the appropriateness to specific tasks
Standard: Students use critical thinking skills to plan and conduct research, manage projects, solve problems, and make informed decisions using appropriate digital tools and resources.
  Benchmark: collect and analyze data to identify solutions and/or make informed decisions
Standard: Students understand human, cultural, and societal issues related to technology and practice legal and ethical behavior.
  Benchmark: exhibit a positive attitude toward using technology that supports collaboration, learning, and productivity
Standard: Students demonstrate a sound understanding of technology concepts, systems, and operations.
  Benchmark: understand and use technology systems

www.ingramcontent.com/pod-product-compliance
Lightning Source LLC
Chambersburg PA
CBHW081152090426
42736CB00017B/3291

* 9 7 8 0 5 7 8 1 0 7 7 4 5 *